NEW DIRECTIONS
FOR INSTITUTIONAL
RESEARCH

Number 30 • 1981

NEW DIRECTIONS
FOR INSTITUTIONAL
RESEARCH

A Quarterly Sourcebook
Marvin W. Peterson, Editor-in-Chief
Sponsored by the Association for Institutional Research

Number 30, 1981

Coping with Faculty Reduction

Stephen R. Hample
Editor

Jossey-Bass Inc., Publishers
San Francisco • Washington • London

COPING WITH FACULTY REDUCTION
New Directions for Institutional Research
Volume VIII, Number 2, 1981
   Stephen R. Hample, Editor

Copyright © 1981 by Jossey-Bass Inc., Publishers
                and
         Jossey-Bass Limited

Copyright under International, Pan American, and Universal Copyright Conventions. All rights reserved. No part of this issue may be reproduced in any form—except for brief quotation (not to exceed 500 words) in a review or professional work—without permission in writing from the publishers.

New Directions for Institutional Research (publication number USPS 098-830) is published quarterly by Jossey-Bass Inc., Publishers, and is sponsored by the Association for Institutional Research. Subscriptions are available at the regular rate for institutions, libraries, and agencies of $30 for one year. Individuals may subscribe at the special professional rate of $18 for one year. *New Directions* is numbered sequentially—please order extra copies by sequential number. The volume and issue numbers above are included for the convenience of libraries. Second-class postage rates paid at San Francisco, California, and at additional mailing offices.

Correspondence:
Subscriptions, single-issue orders, change of address notices, undelivered copies, and other correspondence should be sent to *New Directions* Subscriptions, Jossey-Bass Inc., Publishers, 433 California Street, San Francisco, California 94104.

Editorial correspondence should be sent to the Editor-in-Chief, Marvin W. Peterson, Center for the Study of Higher Education, University of Michigan, Ann Arbor, Michigan 48109.

Library of Congress Catalogue Card Number LC 80-84286

International Standard Serial Number ISSN 0271-0579

International Standard Book Number ISBN 87589-842-4

Cover design by Willi Baum

Manufactured in the United States of America

Contents

Editor's Notes   Stephen R. Hample   vii

Public Policy in an Uncertain Future   Wayne R. Kirschling   1
     Because the public views higher education differently from other institutions, public policy for and reaction to faculty reductions will be unique.

Should You Starve All Programs   Edward A. Dougherty   9
or Eliminate a Few?
     Most administrators approach program reduction as a budget issue; in reality, it is a governance and planning issue of major importance for the 1980s.

Legal Aspects of Faculty Reduction   Robert M. Hendrickson   25
     A well-designed data base, carefully defined procedures, and consultation with legal counsel can greatly reduce the prospect of costly litigation associated with retrenchment.

What if the Faculty Member to Be   Colleen Dolan-Greene   37
Laid Off Is the Governor's Brother?
     Diplomacy and political sophistication are as important as sound data and thorough review in the faculty layoff process.

Budgeting for Retrenchment   Wm. A. Johnstone   63
     The issues surrounding faculty reduction will require increasing sophistication in planning and budgeting. The institutional research professional must play a central role.

Escape Routes: Do They Exist?   Fred F. Harcleroad   79
     It is important to attempt to alleviate the effects of faculty cutbacks through the use of creative methods to hire new faculty, the development of alternative career opportunities for faculty, and unique retirement schemes.

Faculty Retrenchment: The Experience of   Cyrena Pondrom   97
The University of Wisconsin System
     An examination of recent experiences in the varied institutions of The University of Wisconsin System suggests valuable lessons regarding the impact of various approaches to faculty reduction.

Conclusion: Developing a Process to   Homer C. Rose, Jr.   113
Deal with Potential Faculty Reduction   Stephen R. Hample
  Based on recent experience, the essays in this volume suggest lessons and strategies for the institutional researcher dealing with faculty reduction.

Index   125

The Association for Institutional Research was created in 1966 to benefit, assist, and advance research leading to improved understanding, planning, and operation of institutions of higher education. Publication policy is set by its Publications Board.

PUBLICATIONS BOARD
Gerald W. McLaughlin (Chairperson), Virginia Polytechnic Institute and
  State University
Alfred A. Cooke, Institute for Service to Education, Washington, D.C.
John A. Lucas, William Rainey Harper College, Palatine, Illinois
Marilyn McCoy, National Center for Higher Education Management Systems,
  Boulder, Colorado
Marvin W. Peterson, University of Michigan
Joan S. Stark, University of Michigan

EX-OFFICIO MEMBERS OF THE PUBLICATIONS BOARD
Mary E. Corcoran, University of Minnesota
Charles Elton, University of Kentucky
Douglas Mathewson, University of Nevada
Richard R. Perry, University of Toledo

EDITORIAL ADVISORY BOARD
All members of the Publications Board and:
Frederick E. Balderston, University of California, Berkeley
Howard R. Bowen, Claremont Graduate School
Roberta D. Brown, Arkansas College
Robert M. Clark, University of British Columbia
Lyman A. Glenny, University of California, Berkeley
David S. P. Hopkins, Stanford University
Roger G. Schroeder, University of Minnesota
Robert J. Silverman, Ohio State University
Martin A. Trow, University of California, Berkeley

Editor's Notes

Faculty reductions pose a clear and present danger to many institutions. Projected enrollment decline, especially in the New England states, portends a decline in faculty employment. Shortages in state revenue have recently forced cuts at public institutions in Oregon, Utah, and other states. Michigan public institutions recently faced both lower appropriations caused by a local economic crisis and concurrently greater danger from a "Proposition 13" election issue. Recently, the University of Colorado experienced imposed enrollment ceilings, tuition changes, program terminations, and other actions as the legislature attempted to limit enrollment in Boulder and to shore up declining enrollments at other campuses (Jedamus, 1980). As these notes are being written, the editor's own campus has unexpectedly been targeted for faculty reduction because of reporting errors in comparing this campus to peer institutions in a new formula budget process.

Terminated faculty members are obviously directly and severely affected by such conditions. Non-terminated faculty members and others in the campus community are also greatly affected by a decline in campus morale evidenced by interdepartmental budget battles, the push for faculty unionization, votes of no confidence in the campus administration, and dissatisfaction on the part of students denied access to cancelled classes or programs. Campus administrators must not only respond to these problems but also take steps to ensure the vitality of the remaining faculty and to accomplish all this in a manner that can easily and quickly be defended against lawsuits brought by those who will inevitably be displaced.

There is hope. Recent enrollment forecasts are not as bleak as those made a few years ago. Higher education can be flexible and avoid some reduction through new academic programs and administrative procedures. Those institutions that can best survive this period will be able to attract outstanding faculty and emerge from the 1980s in a position of relative strength. However, numerous pitfalls stand in the way of achieving this goal. This volume shares the experience and practical advice of qualified authors and gives suggestions for developing a process to cope most effectively with faculty reduction. Although the problem of faculty reduction is presented from a general administrative viewpoint, each author has attempted to specify the role of institutional research in developing that process.

George H. Callcott, an historian and former vice-chancellor for academic affairs, and David S. Sparks, a vice-chancellor for graduate studies and research, both at the University of Maryland, recently wrote on excellence in higher education. They observed that if money is necessary for quality, it is not sufficient by itself; that leadership is a factor that certainly counts for excellence, but that the modern president must often be more mediator than guide; that the history of the institution is a factor; and that there are two final determinants of excellence: morale and will. They describe morale as follows:

> Morale means an institution's belief in itself, its self-image, its pride. Morale is what Harvard and Virginia faculty have when they feign ignorance of civilization beyond the campus limits: it is what Cornell and Princeton alumni have when they attend reunions, grow misty-eyed at the old college songs, and acknowledge in their wills the source of their success. It is what parents in Texas and Oklahoma feel when they refuse to consider sending their children to colleges outside the state, or what South Carolina and Nebraska have when road signs welcome visitors at the state borders to the land of the Gamecocks or the Cornhuskers. The institution that believes it is better than it is is halfway to being there. The institution that is actually better than it thinks degrades itself.
>
> Morale works among disciplines: it gives mathematics, philosophy, and medicine, for example, their insufferable arrogance; and it allows physicists and historians, who can't find jobs, to feel superior to engineers and business majors who can. Morale is the product of past achievements, further serving to make the past such a strong determinant of excellence. ... Morale flourishes more in small institutions than in large, and it often thrives on hardship. It benefits from able leadership, and maybe from winning football teams. When institutions are divided by controversy, however, morale disintegrates. Chicago suffered from its curriculum wars of the 1930s, and Berkeley, Columbia, and Wisconsin have suffered especially from the student revolts of the 1960s.
>
> Morale is more than the self-esteem of a good salary and professional recognition: it lies more deeply in the confidence

that one is pouring one's professional career into something that is worthwhile and just, serving a cause larger than one's self. Morale is related to morals and morality. It belongs to the faculty member who labors for more than his salary and recognition. For the teacher, it means genuine belief in the utility of teaching. For the scholar, morale is the honest search for truth, apart from rewards or acclaim, because of the belief that one's career is personal, but it exists more deeply in some institutions than in others. Its abundance is a measure of institutional excellence [Callcott and Sparks, 1980, p. 12].

Perhaps protection of campus morale should be the chief goal of administrators facing faculty reductions. I am indebted to the authors who share their experiences here and suggest aspects of a process to strive toward that goal.

Stephen R. Hample
Editor

References

Callcott, G. H. "The Costs of Excellence." *University of Maryland Graduate School Chronicle,* April 1980.
Callcott, G. H., and Sparks, D. S. "Excellence in Higher Education." *The Green Sheet,* Circular Letter No. 13, September 30, 1980, pp. 10-13. (Published by the National Association of State Universities and Land-Grant Colleges, Washington, D.C.)
Jedamus, P. "Legislative Action: The Possibility of Instant Retrenchment." *The Journal of the College and University Personnel Association,* 1980, *31* (1), 38-46.

Stephen R. Hample is the director of institutional research at Montana State University and was formerly with The Maryland State Board of Higher Education. He recently directed a sponsored conference on future faculty employment problems and assisted the Montana Commissioner's Office in creating a statewide faculty development program.

Faculty employment is dependent not only on demographic developments and institutional actions but also on the direction of public policy and the actions of the faculty.

Public Policy in an Uncertain Future

Wayne R. Kirschling

The Ambivalent 1980s

The spring run-off from our high schools will no longer fill all our higher education institutions. This prospect has evoked a growing number of studies, discussions, and conferences. Various experts have suggested conflicting predictions that higher education enrollments might drop precipitously, hold steady, or even grow by as much as 50 percent. Forecasts have been made that alarming numbers of certain types of schools (for example, small, nonselective private colleges with no endowments, located in rural locations) will be forced either to close or to lose their identities through mergers or public takeovers, and that many other institutions (for example, nonselective, comprehensive public colleges) will be especially hard-hit by the impending shortage of college-age youth.

As a result of pessimistic projections, hand-wringing by faculty and administrators is widespread. But this troubled perspective is not the whole story. Other, more positive perspectives on the significance of the reduced number of young adults are beginning to emerge.

The perspective of potential students is important. As the Carnegie Council and others before them have noted, the next two decades promise to be a "golden age" for students. Admission to college and programs of student's first choice will be easier; assistance—financial, academic, and personal—will increase; and graduates will receive more and better job offers.

Another perspective is that of tax and tuition payers. While the appetite for public funds on the part of public institutions (for example, state appropriations for operating purposes) and private institutions (for example, state and federal appropriations for student aid) will remain hearty, the growth in public spending is likely to be moderated by enrollment realities. Any such moderation will undoubtedly be welcomed by taxpayers.

In summary, during the next decade institutions will struggle, some very little and some not successfully; the needs and wants of prospective and enrolled students will receive a great deal more attention; and taxpayers can realistically hope that the higher education share of the state budget (but certainly not the total and per unit costs of higher education) may decline.

But what about the faculty? Few faculty members will be personally buoyed by the "golden" prospects of students, and the welfare of many faculty members will not be synonymous with institutional welfare. For example, tenured professors in high-student-demand programs will have much better employment prospects than untenured instructors in low-student-demand programs, regardless of the enrollment prospects of the institution. Irrespective of institutional circumstances, professors who attract large numbers of enthusiastic students to their classes or large amounts of outside research money will be less concerned about faccuity reductions than faculty who attract neither students nor dollars.

The prospects of the faculty, then, do not necessarily parallel the prospects of students or institutions and are best considered separately. The remainder of this chapter is devoted to some of the circumstances that will affect faculty reductions. Circumstances are considered both from the perspective of public policy and from the perspective of the faculty. These two perspectives are intended to complement the institutional perspectives detailed by the other authors in this volume.

A Shifting Focus in Public Policy

To date, public policy at both the state and federal levels has been oriented more to institutions and students than to faculty. A predictable consequence of impending enrollment declines is that public officials will find themselves gravitating toward issues of faculty employment. This gravitation will happen in several ways.

Faculty as Public Employees. States differ a great deal in their involvement in faculty affairs. Some states, such as Indiana, make it clear that the number of faculty employed and their terms of employment are the responsibility of the trustees of each of the public institutions. Other states, such as Colorado, involve themselves through the budget process in employment details, such as the number of faculty who shall be employed in each program in each public institution, and their work loads and compensation. Still other states involve themselves in faculty employment issues by assuming responsibility for collective bargaining with the faculty. For example, in New Jersey, the governor's office negotiates faculty contracts.

Most states, therefore, have assumed some degree of responsibility for faculty members. It is likely that in more and more states, faculty employment issues brought about by enrollment reductions will finally be decided, not at the departmental or institutional levels, but at the state level. Hence, in the next decade or so there will be a tempting opportunity for the state-level political process to mold and shape a very vulnerable faculty to an unprecedented degree.

The Public Interest in Program Viability. Many states currently concern themselves with academic programs. State funding is often tied to programs, and new and existing programs often are scrutinized by one or more state agencies. As enrollments decline, state level programmatic concerns will expand. In some cases the concern will be that academic featherbedding is diluting the quality of instructional and support programs and diverting resources from the maintenance of facilities and equipment. A second concern may very well be whether institutional responses to enrollment declines will encourage attrition, not among marginal or surplus faculty, but among the best or the most needed faculty. Another concern will be whether reductions in the faculty will leave a series of emaciated programs with too few core staff. Each of these programmatic concerns will provide additional incentives for states to extend their involvement in the staffing decisions of public institutions.

The Opportunity for Manipulating Access. In the last two decades, widespread concerns about access and choice have prompted the introduction of public policy instruments, such as need-based student aid and open admissions, designed to make public and private higher education institutions more available. Ironically, these same instruments may be used to reduce access and choice in the next two decades. For example, at least one state has already considered the imposition of enrollment ceilings and the redirection of student aid appropriations in the public sector as a means of encouraging more enrollments in less attractive public institutions. Other states have eliminated the out-of-state portability of their state-administered student aid. Obviously, such manipulations are inherently in conflict with the expansion of access and choice.

Given the high fixed costs of operating public institutions, there are strong efficiency incentives to keep these institutions operating at or near full capacity. Moreover, in some states the added costs in state-supported student aid of students in private colleges may be higher than the marginal costs of supporting these same students in public institutions operating below capacity. Such considerations may well help weaken the current political resolve to fund student aid programs that provide the student with a choice between public and independent institutions.

Pocketbook Issues. Faculty unemployment touches not only the individuals involved but also their communities and the state. In many communities, higher education is a major industry. In some states, especially those that import a great many students, higher education has statewide significance as a major industry. Even in Indiana, where higher education is not a dominant industry and attracts, as compared to many other states, only modest numbers of out-of-state students, the fiscal impact of higher education on both individual communities and the state is impressive. A student budget of $5,000 would suggest that the 230,000 students in Indiana represent over a $1 billion direct addition to the economy. The 10,000 students who represent the *net* immigration to Indiana represent a $50 million direct addition to the economy. Quite clearly, if states such as Indiana were to experience a 25 percent decline in enrollments, as some have suggested, the fiscal impacts on institutions, communities, and the state would be significant.

As institutional enrollments drop and faculty layoffs begin, it is inevitable that closings and bail-out options will be discussed. Public bail-outs of any enterprise, once unthinkable, have now become acceptable—even sought after. In just a few years, public bail-outs have been applied to cities (for example, New York), corporations (for example, Chrysler), and large scale entrepreneurs (for example, the Hunt brothers). It is too early to predict whether bail-outs will prevail over closings as states begin to struggle with significant enrollment declines. That endangered faculty and institutions will tug at public purse strings seems certain; whether the public will help remains to be seen. Important precedents will be set in the next several years.

An Agenda for the Faculty

The last two decades of growth in higher education cannot be credited to the faculty. Rather than being the source of growth, the faculty has been a direct beneficiary. For most of this period, professors were a scarce resource and their prospects brightened considerably. Compensation increased faster than the rate of inflation; jobs became plentiful and professors were aggressively recruited; and program offerings expanded and graduate education grew enormously, providing professors with a ready audience for their increasingly specialized knowledge. Exceptionally able persons were attracted to the faculty. Once on the faculty, professors worked hard to meet the needs of their students, to contribute to their institutions, and to advance their disciplines and their own professional standings.

Likewise, the potential reductions of the next two decades cannot be attributed to the faculty. Rather than being the cause, the faculty may well view themselves as the victims. The faculty needs to eschew this victim mentality and adopt a strategy for shaping the destiny of higher education.

Being Realistic About Public Sympathy. The prospect of significant numbers of faculty layoffs is unlikely to garner much sympathy in the non-academic community. There will be no national security issues at stake; layoffs will be scattered across the country at more than 3,000 sites; professors, being among the most able and highly educated of our citizens, will be expected to help themselves; and many faculty members will be viewed, not as local persons, but as transient, elite professionals.

The American people are used to layoffs. The current recession, along with earlier economic downswings, has accustomed the country to sharp cutbacks in the private sector work force. Americans seem to accept the idea that jobs cannot be maintained if sales drop.

If jobs are being lost to technology or to foreign competition, or if a plant is being underutilized while new jobs are being created in new plants located elsewhere, then layoffs seem to be less acceptable. However, none of these circumstances apply to the impending enrollment reduction in higher education. Hence, faculty layoffs in most cases will generate little public sympathy and certainly no significant support for unnecessary public expenditures to maintain academic jobs.

Moreover, concern about academic unemployment will have to compete for public attention with a host of other social needs. While it is true that unemployment will be on the public agenda, it is more likely that this will focus upon the unemployment of youth, factory workers, and refugees.

Self Inflicted Injuries. Nationally, the traditional college age cohort is expected to decline 20 to 25 percent in the next twenty years. In the face of the aggregate decline, some institutions will maintain their current enrollments and a few will even show significant enrollment increases. This means that the enrollment shortfall of some institutions is going to be considerably greater than the average. Which institutions are most vulnerable? As noted earlier, there has been considerable speculation on this subject. To date, little attention has been paid to the deleterious effects that the faculty can have upon enrollments. As each institution feels the demographic tremors, a series of faculty reductions will be triggered. The nature of these reactions will have a great deal to do with determining the enrollment prospects of an individual institution.

The growth of higher education has not been accompanied by an equivalent growth in institutional distinctiveness. Most institutions have close competitors—close in program offerings, in pricing, in ease of attending, in image, and in composition of the student body. Hence, an institution that falters, that hurts itself, should expect to lose a significant number of its students. Americans will continue to support winners. Institutions losing enrollments will have to work hard to retain a winning image.

How might an institution, and especially its faculty, injure its own cause? One way would be to lower its standards—its standards of both faculty and student effort and accomplishment. Students, parents, and taxpayers face costs of $3,000 to $10,000 for each full year of a student's education. In return for this considerable sum, they expect an education of high quality.

A second way in which a faculty can harm its cause is by public bickering. For example, while votes of "no confidence" and bitter strikes may serve short-run interests, in the long run they cannot help but blur even the once popular image of higher education institutions as places apart, staffed by special people.

Things Faculty Should Insist Upon. The above discussion is not intended to suggest that the faculty should retire from the stage

—quite the contrary. Faculty members should be in the forefront of insisting that institutional standards be maintained and enhanced at every opportunity. Equally important, the faculty needs to insist that nonviable programs be eliminated as quickly as is consistent with student interests. To do otherwise is to invite continued subsidy of weak programs, a subsidy that will choke off new programs and slowly strangle existing ones.

In addition, the faculty should insist upon action-oriented institutional planning. Since an institution's legal and moral responsibilities to students and faculty in terminated programs cannot be quickly discharged, it is important that planning be used to provide as much lead time as possible. Without planning, painful program terminations are apt to be bungled, with further legal and psychological costs to all concerned.

The faculty needs to become actively involved in institutional planning processes. For example, the faculty should insist upon access to planning data. Planning should not be a hoarding of facts. Rather, it should be a gathering of facts, an identification of alternatives, a clarification of values and issues, a process of dialogue, and a preparation for careful decisions by institutional trustees. The faculty should insist upon such a process and involve themselves in it.

In all matters, the faculty should insist that there be no procedural surprises. Procedures that carefully spell out roles, responsibilities, and prerogatives in reductions of staff should now be in place. If they are not, their development should be a high priority for the faculty.

Finally, the faculty should insist upon honesty and straightforwardness—from their members, the administration, and trustees. Nothing will infect a relationship more quickly than a discovery, or even a strong suspicion, of dishonesty. The standard of honesty is one that is widely cherished in higher education; it is essential for research and the foundation of the instructional process.

Concluding Thoughts

Higher education is fortunate: It has a rich history of major contributions to society; it employs some of society's most talented members; and it enjoys widespread confidence, even awe, from the lay community. Even if enrollments decline, higher education needs to remind itself that its cup is almost full, rather than a bit empty.

Studies, including recent ones, have repeatedly shown that a high proportion of faculty are happy with their chosen profession. Yet the profession is caught up in larger changes that will alter its nature and decrease its membership. Hence, individual faculty members are well advised to do more personal planning. Too many have grown used to the security their degrees and positions have provided them. Many faculty would benefit from preparing for an alternative career, whether in higher education or elsewhere, even though most faculty will never need to exercise such an option.

It may yet happen that the academic profession will elude the demographic reaper. But it is not likely. Hence, it is important that the academic employment discussion move beyond demographics. This discussion has been an attempt to do this by suggesting that both public policy and faculty members themselves have important roles to play in determining faculty employment.

Wayne R. Kirschling is deputy director of the Indiana Commission for Higher Education. He was editor of the recently published Jossey-Bass sourcebook, Evaluating Faculty Performance and Vitality. *Prior to assuming his current responsibilities, he was an associate director of the National Center for Higher Education Management Systems (NCHEMS).*

Most administrators approach program reduction as a budget issue; in reality, it is a governance and planning issue of major importance for the 1980s.

Should You Starve All Programs or Eliminate a Few?

Edward A. Dougherty

At a recent staff meeting, the academic vice-president of a major university asked the institutional research director to prepare a list of academic programs that could be eliminated if the governor carried out his threat of major cuts in the higher education appropriation. There was an almost audible groan from the staff, and after the meeting the director confided that he had prepared such a list several years ago under similar circumstances, but it had never been used. Instead, the academic vice-president made cuts across the board. The director fully expected that the same pattern would be followed again this time: there would be lots of talk, but no programs would be cut. Undoubtedly, similar scenarios could be written about many colleges and universities across the country.

Why is there so much talk about program discontinuance and so little action? There can be clear advantages to closing one program for the sake of improving the quality and resources available to the remaining programs, but there are also both ideational and practical reasons why such action is so difficult.

With respect to ideational or attitudinal reasons, Donald Michael (1968) points out that society is not ready to accept no-growth, decline, and defeat. After centuries of expansion, Americans have been socialized to expect growth. They now find it difficult to accept gloomier prospects. On an organizational level, one will find obstacles to accepting the idea of closing a program. Herbert Kaufman (1971) talks about the limits of organizational change, pointing out that value is placed in organizational stability, not change. There is a fear of the unknown and an attitude that environmental change should be met with addition, not substitution or subtraction. Cameron (1978) points out that changes in public health policy are difficult because of ideological inertia. Such inertia tends to support existing policy, and any new ideology must be strong enough to overcome the inertia of an old ideology. All of these factors—social unpreparedness, organizational obstacles, and ideological inertia—make any change difficult, and radical change such as program discontinuance even more difficult.

In addition to ideational reasons for resisting program discontinuance, there are also a variety of practical reasons that make discontinuance problematic. Melchiori (1980), Deleon (1978), and Bardach (1976) discuss both ideational and practical obstacles to program discontinuance. On the practical side they cite legal barriers, the lack of incentives to close programs, the inevitable formation of anti-termination coalitions that must be dealt with, governance and political structures that must be worked through, the lack of agreement about what constitutes quality, inconsistent procedures, and economic, social, and political uncertainty. Given these obstacles, it is little wonder that discontinuance may be much talked about but rarely implemented. Yet it is something that every administrator and faculty member will have to face in the 1980s, if one trusts the demographic and economic forecasts for higher education.

This chapter will examine several aspects of program discontinuance in order to help the college or university administrator who is seriously considering the discontinuance of an academic program. Most people approach discontinuance as a budget issue, and the question of discontinuance is most often raised when budget reductions are projected. Discontinuance may reduce expenditures in the long run, but it is unlikely to help with a short-term budget crisis. Rather, discontinuance should be approached as a governance process that requires extensive, rational planning before being undertaken. The following sections describe the steps in that process and some of the pitfalls that should be avoided. This advice is based on a national study of discontinuance conducted by the author with the support of the Exxon Foundation.

Under What Circumstances Should Programs Be Closed?

Many factors go into the decision to discontinue an academic program, not the least of which is economic. But if we are to look at program discontinuance in the broader context of governance and planning, then three factors tend to dominate. They are: (1) the academic quality of the program under consideration, (2) the changing environment in which higher education must operate, and (3) the changing priorities of the institution or state. The following three examples will illustrate these factors.

Academic Quality. In 1973, the University of California at Berkeley discontinued the School of Criminology on the basis of qualitative factors. There was a protest of the closure by the students in the program and some student government leaders, but, on the whole, the campus accepted the decision as a fair one based on qualitative factors carefully studied by a highly regarded review team. In December 1972, the graduate dean established a review committee to "inquire into all aspects of the Criminology degree programs." The dean had questions about the quality of programs. For example, the school was not following standard procedures for doctoral examinations, and complaints had been filed by faculty outside the school about the quality of dissertations.

The review committee did an extremely thorough job during its six months of deliberations, making wide use of information from both the graduate school and the School of Criminology itself. The committee met with school faculty, received written comments from recent graduates, and read recent dissertations. The review committee identified as the core problem of the school the inability to develop a curriculum to meet its own standards of providing both professional and academic approaches to the field of criminology. The committee argued that the school was not meeting the standards of quality expected of a professional school at Berkeley. It had failed to combine professional training of high quality with academic training and research of high quality. The issue was not one of failure to *do* academic training research, but of pursuing that end in a narrow and isolated fashion removed from contact with the professional field. The question of quality, then, was linked to the question of program definition, at least at the graduate level.

At the undergraduate level, the committee noted that the curriculum lacked coherence as a major. It was made up of a series of largely unrelated subjects of current concern to the students. There were no prerequisites for any of the courses, and no theoretical synthesis was provided in a "cap-stone" course. Admission was not selective at the undergraduate level; at the graduate level, it was based on a quota system of 50 percent minority and 50 percent female. In the final analysis, the school did not meet the qualitative standards expected of a professional school at Berkeley. This failure of standards was carefully documented by the review committee and was supported by the graduate dean and chancellor.

Changing Environment. The State University of New York (SUNY) at Albany provides an illustration of a second factor in program discontinuance: the changing environment in which higher education must operate. Albany discontinued twenty-six programs and released eighty-eight faculty, thirty of whom were tenured. This action was taken, in large part, because Albany had built a series of programs, especially at the doctoral level, in expectation that it would grow into a major research university. It found itself caught during expansion by declining budgets and enrollments, especially at the doctoral level.

Albany was catapulted from a small teachers college of 3,800 to a university center of 14,000 students in a period of less than fifteen years. Doctoral programs grew from two to twenty-nine. A new campus was built to hold nearly 20,000, with room for expansion. By 1972, the state master plan reduced Albany's projected enrollment ceiling, and by 1975 the first of two major budget cuts came, forcing the administration to cut forty faculty positions. Additional cuts were made in the budget and in faculty later in 1975 and again in 1976. The striking thing about the Albany case is that they alone of all the state universities made actual program cuts. Other units in the state suffered similar budget tightening, but Albany was the only state university to cut programs voluntarily. Other universities implemented their reductions largely by attrition. Other academic programs may have been cut as a result of actions taken by the State Education Department, but only Albany had a system of program reviews and a decision-making mechanism in place with which to cut programs and faculty positions quickly enough to meet the changing economic situation in which they found themselves.

The Albany case has been reviewed elsewhere (Shirley and Volkwein, 1978; American Association of University Professors,

1977; Mingle, 1978) and will not be discussed in detail here. It is significant, however, because the university was able to respond to both gradual changes (shifting enrollments) and sudden changes (budget cuts) in the environment through a series of well executed program closures.

Changing Priorities. The third factor that is significant in considering program discontinuance in a broader context is the changing priorities of an institution or state agency for higher education. The University of Pennsylvania discontinued its School of Allied Medical Professions primarily on the basis of a priority decision that the school did not sufficiently fit the preferred model for the university. The school offered only an undergraduate program without graduate offerings and without a research emphasis appropriate to the University of Pennsylvania. Concern was expressed that the faculty did not have the resources at its disposal to establish graduate programs and develop a research capability, but there was never any question that the faculty was qualified to do the job. The school was ranked among the top two or three schools of allied health in the country. The administration felt, however, that the mission of the school was not appropriate to the university.

Through an open process of discussion, formal mechanisms of review, and extensive involvement of the trustees, the vice-president for Health Affairs was able to gain approval for phasing out the school. In addition to the priority factor influencing the decision, there was also an indirect financial factor. The university was not under undue financial pressure at the time the decision was made, but it was committed to reducing the scope of its operation over the long run. The administration also recognized that to make the School of Allied Medical Professions into a school compatible with the mission of the university would take nearly a 50 percent increase in the school's budget. The university did not have the resources to make that kind of commitment and was unwilling to continue the school in its present state.

These three brief illustrations show that, while there may be three primary factors influencing program discontinuance, they do not operate alone, nor do they operate without influence from a variety of other factors. The question of when to consider program discontinuance may be answered by concern about quality or changing environments or priorities. There may also be many other factors, especially economic and demographic, which will lead institutions to consider program discontinuance seriously. If that decision is made, what should be done next? The following sections will address that question.

The Review Process

Whether consideration of academic program discontinuance is for qualitative, environmental, or priority reasons, the review process is perhaps the single most important step in the sequence of events. If the review is done adequately, it will give a fair assessment of quality. It will also allow decisions to be made about programs if environmental factors pressure the institution, and it will allow a ranking of programs based on how well they fit overall institutional goals. An adequate review process will also help in dealing with the antidiscontinuance coalition that inevitably will arise if discontinuance is announced as a serious possibility. Without an adequate review, the whole prospect of discontinuance will be jeopardized.

There are four basic questions concerning program review: Who has the authority to review? What programs will be reviewed? What criteria will be used? And, what procedures will be most appropriate to the situation?

The Question of Authority. Virtually everyone claims authority for program review—the faculty, campus administrators, the graduate dean, the external coordinating board, even the legislature. Looking at program discontinuance in the broader context of government planning, it is essential that the lines of authority be clearly understood at the outset. Only then can rational planning take place. Looking at the institutions that have considered or implemented program discontinuance reveals that no one pattern of authority prevails. Several of the institutions studied centered the concern for discontinuance at the graduate level, and the graduate dean had the authority to conduct reviews. This pattern was the one begun at Berkeley in the review of criminology, but after that graduate school committee began, it was asked by the faculty senate to look at the undergraduate programs also. (The faculty senate had authority for review of undergraduate programs.) Such cooperation between those with authority to review graduate and undergraduate programs may not always prevail. For example, two separate review procedures were set up at the Riverside campus of the University of California.

At the University of Michigan, the authority for review rests with the deans of the various schools and colleges and the academic vice-president. Reviews are usually timed to correspond with the ending of a term appointment of a department chairman or dean, providing the administration with the opportunity to make personnel changes if warranted by the outcome of the review. Such personnel changes may be viewed as an alternative to discontinuance.

The question of authority becomes more complex if agencies outside the institution claim authority for program review. For example, the situation at Albany became more complex because the regents and the State Education Department claimed authority to review and "deregister" doctoral programs. The institution and the regents were involved in a major court battle when the department recommended deregistration of doctoral programs in history and in English. The campus representatives felt that these programs were essential to the core of the university, but the courts decided that the regents did have authority to register and deregister programs.

The Albany situation points out the importance of clarifying the question of authority for program discontinuance. Most campuses and state agencies have informal understandings about who will review programs, but as questions of discontinuance become more central to the life of higher education, these informal agreements may be challenged and more formal procedures may have to be adopted.

What Programs Should Be Reviewed? In his discussion of strategies for program discontinuance, Robert Berdahl (1975) points out the need to select a few programs that can be evaluated in depth within the capacity of the group doing the reviews. To review on a more massive basis results in either an overloaded review board or great superficiality, or both. Institutions studied by this author show both extremes of overwork and superficiality. In the state of Washington, nearly all Ph.D. programs were reviewed at once. An initial audit of academic programs identified units with low-degree productivity. A second audit identified nearly 300 duplicate programs that were subsequently all reviewed at the same time. Only quantitative measures were used to judge programs, and many faculty criticized the process as superficial and unproductive.

A more typical pattern is the use of quantitative indicators to select programs that may require more detailed reviews. Indicators such as student credit-hour productivity or the number of degrees awarded may trigger a more thorough review. The assumption should not be made, however, that only negative indicators are used to select programs for review. Many administrators prefer to select both strong and weak programs for review in order to avoid the assumption by faculty that reviews will only be used for programs an administrator would like to discontinue. The states of New York, Louisiana, and Florida review their programs in common disciplinary clusters. For example, all the nursing programs in Florida were reviewed at once by outside evaluators. Some institutions will review programs in common clusters, such as natural sciences, social sciences, or humanities. Finally, there will always be a need for *ad hoc* reviews as issues arise, such as the review of criminology at Berkeley.

Like the question of authority, the question of what program should be reviewed has no single answer. The important thing is to use a selection method that is agreed upon by all those affected so that no one can make a charge of capricious or arbitrary action. Ideally, program review should be an ongoing part of the planning cycle so that when action is required, as it was at Albany, review documents are readily available.

The Question of Criteria. James Mingle (1978) identifies two types of reviews that can be distinguished on the basis of the type of criteria used for evaluating programs. One type of review is quantitative and uses measures of evaluation such as degree productivity, faculty work loads, and student credit-hour productivity. The other type of review is qualitative and evaluates programs on the basis of peer judgments about faculty quality, value and character of the program, and the performance of its students. Most reviews will use a combination of numbers and intuition, but differences can be noted in emphasis based on the proximity of the reviewers to the operating unit. For example, there is a tendency for state agencies, which are remote from operating units, to depend more heavily upon quantitative program analysis. Reviews conducted by deans or department chairpersons, however, depend more on peer judgments of quality.

The National Board of Graduate Education (1973) emphasizes that single measures of quality should not be applied to diverse programs, but rather multiple indicators of quality should be developed. The board points out that statewide planners should resist the temptation to apply simplistic formulas to doctoral programs. For example, the board would argue against cutting out any program that has fewer than two graduates per year. Such a measure might be used as a signal for a more thorough review, but it should not be used alone. Viewed from the broader context of governance and planning, regardless of criteria for evaluating programs that might be discontinued, agreement should be reached before any steps are taken.

The Question of Process. What is the most appropriate methodology for program review? Once again, no single pattern is universal. Under the best conditions, the process will be decided in the context of the institutional governance structure and become part of the overall planning process for the institution. The most frequently used process involves some form of peer review. With the exception of closures in the state of Washington, few programs have been terminated without some form of peer review. In many cases, the reviewers are from outside the institution, but they may also be internal, as was the case at Berkeley. The important thing seems to be the development of some professional judgment on the quality of the program.

Dressel (1976) differentiates four types of evaluation according to their aims: (1) planning and development of new programs; (2) aiding decisions about how to use resources (input evaluation); (3) providing feedback about previous decisions (process evaluation); and (4) assessing the attainment of goals (output evaluation). In most cases of program discontinuance, the interest is in output evaluation, but elements of all the other forms of evaluation may also be important, including evaluation for new programs that might substitute for the discontinued program. Dressel says that the evaluation of outputs include the identification of (1) correspondence and discrepancies between original objectives and attainments, (2) unintended results, (3) needed process changes, (4) quality control, and (5) program changes.

Palola and others (1977) and Clark (1979) both suggest the use of measures of academic quality with a variety of sources of information from peers, students, faculty, and alumni. While their aims are different, both authors are looking for more objective methods of program assessment that use a complex system of data collection and criteria. Their procedures are relatively new and untried, but could provide a significant contribution for those interested in reviews that assess multiple program qualities.

The Process of Program Discontinuance

Program review is, of course, just one step in the larger process of program discontinuance. Programs are being reviewed all the time, but they are more likely to change than to be discontinued. If, however, an administrator concludes that program closure is in order, what are the steps that must be taken? Melchiori (1980) points out that there can be four levels of discontinuance: (1) the elimination of a paper program, (2) the release of non-tenured faculty and gradual phasing out of a program, (3) the release of tenured faculty with a future date set for closure, and (4) the immediate release of all faculty and transfer of all students. Each step involves progressively more complex planning and consultation.

The University of Michigan has developed discontinuance guidelines (Davis and Dougherty, 1979) that cover all the stages of Melchiori's scheme. Assurances are given that tenured faculty have never been released at Michigan as a result of program closure, and the maintenance of tenured faculty is among the highest priorities of the university. If it becomes necessary to release tenured faculty, however, every effort will be made to retrain and relocate tenured faculty members. In cases where this is not possible, tenured faculty have rights of appeal described in the regents' bylaws.

Prior to releasing any faculty, the Michigan guidelines spell out an elaborate procedure of reviews, consultations, public hearings, and appeals at both the school or college level and at the level of the vice-president for academic affairs. The procedures are probably not transferable because they follow the unique pattern of governance that has grown out of Michigan's past. The important point is that each institution must develop its own system for handling discontinuance *before* it becomes necessary to use it. Such a system should spell out a series of checks and balances that will make arbitrary action less likely. At Michigan these checks and balances are provided by having dual systems of review and consultation at the school or college level and at the vice-presidential level. This system may be criticized for being cumbersome and time consuming, but it has already been used effectively in two situations, one that resulted in a closure and one in the transfer of a program to another unit. Some have argued that the procedures will not be used again, but if any program is going to be closed at Michigan, either these guidelines or something very similar will have to be used.

A second thing that should be spelled out in discontinuance guidelines is the role of faculty in the program under consideration, the role of governing faculty in the school or college in which the program resides, and the role of the overall university faculty governance group. Michigan's guidelines place each of these groups in advisory and consultive roles rather than in decision-making roles, recognizing that the Board of Regents has the ultimate legal authority to begin and end programs. The same role is given to constituents outside the university who are interested in the program under review. They should be consulted and listened to as valuable advisors, but they should not have veto power.

One should be prepared to deal with the anti-discontinuance coalition that will be formed whenever discontinuance is contemplated. Even a paper program with no students may be the sacred cow of some constituency. Presumably, it was important to someone or it would not be on the books. Dealing with this coalition may involve more than simply seeking their advice. They can become an important political force seeking to influence the final decision-makers (the regents in the case of Michigan), occasionally demonstrating and holding sit-ins at administrative offices. Hence, it is important to be well informed and to keep the final decision-makers well informed.

The Role of Institutional Values

When all the quantitative and qualitative evidence is in, all the hearings held, and all the consultants consulted, the final judgment about discontinuing a program will be based on some sense of institutional values. How does one define those values? Values are the often unstated assumptions that guide the actions of institutions. They are based on past institutional history, connections with the environment, beliefs about the nature of students, faculty and constituencies, and hopes for the future. Good administrators should be able to articulate the institutional values of their colleges or universities. Many pragmatic administrators and analysts are not very comfortable with the notion that values play a role in decision-making. They would prefer to make decisions in a value-free context. Freedom from values may be desirable in the laboratory or in research analysis, but it is impossible to be free of values in selecting topics for research or teaching, in defining measures of quality, in determining what environmental changes to respond to, or in setting priorities. The role of values is important in these areas for both the individual and the institution because, after all, an institution is only as good as its decision-makers—past, present, and future.

Because of the importance of institutional values, it is imperative that institutional representatives work continuously on role and mission statements. As these statements become understood by the academic community, they become translated into programs, curriculums, and policies. Only an understanding of the role and mission of an institution produces wise decisions about what programs to keep, what programs to discontinue, and what programs to add. Role and mission statements are often viewed as something to cover the first page of a college catalogue. As long as that is all they are, then decisions about program discontinuance will be made by the principle of the king's decree. The king—be he dean, president, or the board acting collectively—will decide what to support and what to discontinue. This king may have an intuitive sense of institutional values, so that his decision will be acceptable to most of his subjects, but as with any monarchial structure, the king may lose touch with his subjects and begin making decisions that are acceptable to fewer and fewer people.

An alternative to decision-making by the principle of the king's decree is decision-making by the principle of academic democracy that begins with an articulation of institutional values and proceeds with orderly discussion and planning of academic programming. Academic democracy is different from other kinds of political democracy because there is one final authority, usually the board of trustees. The trustees have the ultimate responsibility for the well-being of the institution, and with that responsibility must go the power to make decisions about academic matters. Fortunately, most boards have delegated their power over academic matters to the faculty, but in matters of program discontinuance, board members will undoubtedly re-establish their authority. Assuming they want to make wise decisions, they will seek the advice and counsel of those affected by their decisions. Their decisions will be improved if the academic community has had a chance to think about and discuss the matter in light of an understanding of academic values. For example, the decision of the board of the University of Pennsylvania to discontinue the School of Allied Medical Practice was made on the basis of an understanding of institutional values about program levels. The value, whether articulated or not, was that programs at the University of Pennsylvania are better off if they are offered at both the undergraduate and graduate levels and involve some research component. The university could tolerate a program that did not have all these components, but as financial pressures mounted, a decision had to be made about what to keep and what to discontinue. If some form of discussion about institutional values relating to program level had taken place, then the decision might have been easier. As it turned out, the faculty senate voted against the discontinuance, but they could accept the decision because the board was reflecting values that were shared by most of the faculty. If there had been some prior discussion of those values, then the decision might have been reached with a larger consensus of the academic community.

Another example of the role of institutional values can be seen in the Berkeley case. The important institutional value in the decision to discontinue the School of Criminology involved a definition of quality. Values deaing with quality are, perhaps, the most difficult and complex to define, but at an institution like Berkeley there is a commonly understood meaning to the term, and most administrators and faculty know when the boundary has been crossed by a program from an acceptable to an unacceptable level of quality. Berkeley could not tolerate a program outside the normal range of institutional qualitative values, and the School of Criminology was closed. In this case, it was the students who protested the decision, which points out the importance of involving student leaders in the discussion of institutional values.

The importance of institutional values in program discontinuance cannot be overemphasized, but one must also recognize, as SUNY-Albany had to recognize, that external factors, such as budget cuts or external coordinating agencies, may force discontinuances that fly in the face of institutional values. The fact that Albany was able to make decisions quickly and smoothly about closing programs suggests that there was fairly wide consensus about institutional values and an appropriate system that could transfer those values into program decisions. The fact that Albany had hired virtually all its faculty within the last fifteen years also suggests that they may have come to the institution with a fairly clear and homogeneous sense of what its values were.

Conclusions

In discussions of program discontinuance, there is a danger of starting a process of self-fulfilling prophecy that may partly account for why there is so much talk about program closure and so little action. If one plans for retrenchment, one gets retrenchment. This attitude is reflected in a recent American Council on Education report (Frances, 1980), which says we should do more creative thinking about opening up new markets to new and old constituencies. There is clearly a need for more creative thinking to offset both population and economic decline in higher education.

It is not desirable that institutions become so "retrenchment-oriented" that they fail to look for creative alternatives. At the same time, new initiatives cannot be expected without the elimination of old programs. There is a need for consideration of program discontinuance that goes well beyond the need for responding to retrenchment. Institutions need to consider discontinuance as a mechanism for maintaining quality. Without any pressure from declining populations or finances, Berkeley closed a program due to quality considerations. Discontinuance can be considered as one response to environmental pressures other than demographic and financial ones. There is a constant shift in the demand for education in the society at large, and institutions that wish to respond to those changes in the environment cannot just keep adding new programs. Eventually, something must go. Finally, discontinuance can be a means of shifting institutional priorities. The University of Pennsylvania discontinued its School of Allied Medical Programs out of recognition that it did not adequately reflect university priorities.

The obstacles to discontinuance are real, but they can be overcome if discontinuance is viewed in the broader context of governance and planning models. It can be facilitated by the presence of an ongoing process of program review. If program review is seen as a routine part of institutional life, then evaluation material is readily available when discontinuance is contemplated or required. Discontinuance can also be facilitated by developing guidelines for program closure *prior* to the time they are actually needed. Few institutions are likely to follow this recommendation, given the pressure of other academic business, but even a few month's lead time of thinking through the process can save an enormous amount of time and trouble later on. If there is anticipation of a possible closure, it is time to start developing these guidelines.

Finally, if program discontinuance is seen as a possibility, it might be worthwhile considering the appointment of a "process manager." Someone who is appointed on a short-term basis to monitor the process could greatly facilitate reaching the best conclusion. Such a person would have to be a neutral party in the controversy and someone trusted by the faculty as a whole. The manager could be directly responsible to the board, but working closely with the entire academic administration. The person holding such a position could assure that the process of program discontinuance is followed in a fair and equitable manner and that discontinuance is seen in its broader governance and planning context.

References

American Association of University Professors. "Report of the Investigating Committee on Academic Freedom and Tenure: The State University of New York." B. Davis, Chairman. *AAUP Bulletin,* 1977, *63* (3), 237-260.

Bardach, E. "Policy Termination as a Political Process." *Policy Sciences*, 1976, 7, 123-131.

Berdahl, R. O. "Criteria and Strategies for Program Discontinuance and Institutional Closure." Paper presented for the Kellogg In-Service Training Seminar, State Higher Education Executive Officers Annual Conference, New Orleans, July 30, 1975.

Cameron, J. M. "Ideology and Policy Termination: Reconstructing California's Mental Health System." In J. May and A. Wildavsky (Eds.), *The Policy Cycle in Politics and Public Policy*. Beverly Hills, Calif.: Sage, 1978.

Clark, M. J. "A Practical Guide to Graduate Program Review." *Findings*, 1979, 5 (1), 1-4.

Davis, C. K., and Dougherty, E. A. "Guidelines for Program Discontinuance." *Educational Record*, 1979, 60 (1), 68-77.

DeLeon, P. "A Theory of Policy Termination." In J. May and A. Wildavsky (Eds.), *The Policy Cycle in Politics and Public Policy*. Beverly Hills, Calif.: Sage, 1978.

Dressel, P. L. *Handbook of Academic Evaluation: Assessing Institutional Effectiveness, Student Progress, and Professional Performance for Decision Making in Higher Education*. San Francisco: Jossey-Bass, 1976.

Frances, C. *College Enrollment: Testing the Conventional Wisdom Against the Facts*. Washington, D.C.: American Council on Education, 1980.

Kaufman, H. *The Limits to Organizational Change*. University: University of Alabama Press, 1971.

Melchiori, G. S. "Patterns of Program Discontinuance: A Comparative Analysis of State Agency Procedures for Initiating and Implementing the Discontinuance of Academic Programs." Unpublished doctoral dissertation, University of Michigan, 1980.

Michael, D. *The Unprepared Society: Planning for a Precarious Future*. New York: Basic Books, 1968.

Mingle, J. R. "Influencing Academic Outcomes: The Power and Impact of Statewide Program Reviews." In J. R. Mingle and others, *The Closing System of Academic Employment*. Atlanta, Ga.: Southern Regional Educational Board, 1978.

National Board of Graduate Education. *Doctoral Manpower Forecasts and Policy*. No. 2. Washington, D.C.: National Board of Graduate Education, 1973.

Palola, E. G., Lehmann, T., Bradley, A. P., Jr., and Debus, R. *PERC Handbook (Program Effectiveness and Related Costs)*. Saratoga Springs, N.Y.: Office of Research and Evaluation, Empire State College, 1977.

Shirley, R. C., and Volkwein, J. F. "Establishing Academic Program Priorities." *Journal of Higher Education*, 1978, 49 (5), 472-488.

Edward A. Dougherty is assistant to the academic vice-president and coordinator for evaluation at the University of Michigan. For the last several years he has been studying the question of program discontinuance with partial support from the Exxon Foundation.

A well designed data base, carefully defined procedures, and consultation with legal counsel can greatly reduce the prospect of costly litigation associated with retrenchment.

Legal Aspects of Faculty Reduction

Robert M. Hendrickson

In legal journals few articles exist on financial exigency as a justifiable reason to lay off tenured faculty. This may be explained in one of two ways. One reason may be that we have seen only the tip of the iceberg and that, as more tenured faculty are laid off as a result of financial exigency, discussion and debate will increase. The second reason may be that there is agreement among the courts and theorists on the appropriateness of a "financial exigency" as a valid reason for removal of tenured faculty and the procedures required to effect that removal. Consistency among the available court cases suggests the latter reason is valid.

This chapter will present the institutional researcher with an introduction to the legal aspects of faculty reduction and will suggest appropriate policies, procedures, and data gathering techniques necessary in the event that a financial exigency arises. First, the nature of the tenure contract will be discussed along with the distinction between public and private institutions. This will include procedural requirements in the termination of contracts as mandated to public institutions through the Fourteenth Amendment. The second section will discuss the legal basis for the financial exigency as an acceptable reason for termination of a tenure contract. The third section will analyze the case law on financial exigency, identifying various issues resolved and procedures outlined by the courts. The fourth section will briefly discuss a recent case on legal liability of public officials involved in the removal of tenured faculty for financial exigencies. Finally, the procedures and data-gathering needs of institutional researchers will be discussed.

Federal case law on the issue was the primary source of information. However, some state cases were included. Although this chapter will focus on public institutions, these issues do have application for private institutions.

The Nature of a Tenure Contract

Tenure is an unintegrated, unilateral, lifetime employment contract. Unintegrated means that not everything is spelled out in the contract document, but that other documents are considered as part of the contract, such as the faculty handbook, college catalog, or board of trustee bylaws and minutes (*Iowa Law Review*, 1976, p. 488). Unilateral, according to *Black's Law Dictionary,* means that one party agrees to the expressed terms of the contract without gaining an "expressed promise or performance" from the other party (1968, p. 397). The university, in this case, offers lifetime employment without defining specific tasks to be performed by the faculty, leaving them greater freedom in fulfilling their teaching and research responsibilities.

Where no specific written document signed by both parties exists and/or since the contract is unilateral, there is question whether a contract really exists. The doctrine of consideration is used to prove the existence of the tenure contract if the following formal functions are present (*Iowa Law Review,* 1976, p. 499). First, tenure is granted either through written notification or through notation in official minutes. Second, the decision is made after a probationary period, based on deliberate evaluation of past performance as a teacher and researcher. Third, the institution's functions of learning and research necessitate this type of contractual relationship in order to further society's interests. Finally, the institution's policies indicate that a tenure decision is one that requires serious deliberation and is made with expectation that it will be long term (1976, p. 500). These provisions are consistent with the purposes of the tenure contract and serve to validate its existence in a court of law.

In private institutions, the written tenure contract, other institutional documents, and previous practices will govern the rights of tenured faculty in cases where a breach of the contract has been alleged. According to Brown (1977, p. 280), "the legal effect of a tenure system is to place restrictions on the power of the employing institutions to terminate tenured professors except for cause after a hearing." A definition of cause and the procedures for the hearing are spelled out in the contract or implied through accepted institutional procedures.

Public institutions, on the contrary, are governed not only by the contract but also by the constitutional prerogatives of the Fourteenth Amendment. The original Bill of Rights deals with a citizen in his relationship with the federal government. The Fourteenth Amendment applied those guarantees to citizens in their relationship with state government. That amendment forbids the state from making any laws which infringe on a person's equal rights protection under the law or the due process of law. Public institutions, as agents of state government, must guarantee these rights to citizens. One of the rights guaranteed was the "pursuit of happiness," which has been interpreted to include a person's need for gainful employment. This means that a job becomes something of value necessary in the pursuit of happiness, making it like property: due process under the Fourteenth Amendment is required when denying a person property ("property interest") (*Black's Law Dictionary*, 1968, p. 382).

Two cases decided in the Supreme Court, *Perry* v. *Sindermann,* 1972, and *Board of Regents* v. *Roth,* 1972, clearly require procedural due process at a public institution where a property interest in the job exists because of an existing implied or written tenure contract (*Perry* v. *Sindermann*), or where other constitutional freedoms (that is, freedom of speech) may be infringed upon as a result of the removal of a non-tenured or tenured faculty member (*Board of Regents* v. *Roth,* 1972). The court states: "Proof of such a property interest would not, of course, entitle him to reinstatement. But such proof would obligate college officials to grant a hearing at his request, where he could be informed of the grounds for his non-retention and challenge their sufficiency" (*Perry* v. *Sindermann,* 1972, 408 U.S. 593, p. 603).

Public institutions have strict requirements to provide due process in the removal of tenured faculty. However, the due process required in the case of removal of financial exigencies, as we will see in the section on case law analysis, is something less than those spelled out above. First, however, it is important to understand the origin of the concept of "financial exigencies" as a legally accepted reason in the layoff of tenured faculty.

Financial Exigency: The Accepted Prerogative

Where a contract or institutional policy specifically states that shortage of funds (financial exigency) may result in the termination of tenured contracts, the courts have honored that statement (*American Association of University Professors* v. *Bloomfield College,* 1974; *Scheuer* v. *Creighton University,* 1977) and have upheld the institution's prerogative to dismiss tenured faculty. However, many institutions have not specifically stated in the tenure contract that financial exigency is a basis for removal of tenured faculty, but have formally adopted or accepted in a published document the American Association of University Professors (AAUP) standards governing tenure. The AAUP 1940 Statement of Principles (*AAUP Bulletin,* 1974, p. 270) states:

- After the expiration of a probationary period, teachers ... should have permanent or continuous tenure, and their service should be terminated only for adequate cause, except in the case of retirement for age, or under extraordinary circumstances because of financial exigency.
- Termination of a continuous appointment because of financial exigency should be demonstrably bonafide.

If this document is incorporated into the contract in the manner above, financial exigency becomes a part of the contract (*Browzin* v. *Catholic University of America,* 1975).

Even if no direct or indirect mention of financial exigency can be found either in the contract or supporting documents, the court has ruled that the prerogative exists because it is common academic practice. In *Krotkoff* v. *Goucher College,* 1978, (585 F. 2d 679), the court cited the AAUP 1940 Policy Statement on Tenure and stated: "The reported cases support the conclusion that tenure is not generally understood to preclude demonstrably *bona fide* dismissal for financial reasons.... In other words, where the contract did not mention this term (financial exigency), the courts construed tenure as implicitly granting colleges the right to make *bona fide* dismissals for financial reasons" (See also *Browzin* v. *Catholic University,* 1975, and *Johnson* v. *Board of Regents of the University of Wisconsin System,* 1974). The court is saying that since the financial exigency rationale has become a part of accepted academic standards in higher education, it is a legal prerogative in the layoff of tenured faculty.

This brings the reader to the issues of defining a financial exigency and the removal procedures in public institutions mandated by Fourteenth Amendment "due process" provisions.

The Case Law on Financial Exigency

The case law on financial exigency presented here comprises primarily federal cases on the issue. All the cases found were decided in the 1970s. This section will explain the court's interpretation of the following issues: defining a *bona fide* financial exigency, identifying the appropriate decision makers, defining appropriate criteria, clarifying due process requirements, and describing the liability issue.

Defining a Bona Fide Financial Exigency. The courts have defined an appropriate financial exigency as an existing deficit in the institution's operating budget (*American Association of University Professors* v. *Bloomfield College*, 1974; *Krotkoff* v. *Goucher College*, 1978). The courts have also held that legislative reductions in the operating budget constitute a *bona fide* financial exigency (*Brenna* v. *Southern Colorado State College*, 1978; *Johnson* v. *Board of Regents of the University of Wisconsin System*, 1975; *Klein* v. *The Board of Higher Education of the City of New York*, 1977). They have also held that the financial exigency need not exist in the institution as a whole, but rather can be limited to a single academic unit, such as a college or department (*Brenna* v. *Southern Colorado State College*, 1978). In *Scheuer* v. *Creighton University*, 1977, (260 N.W.2d 631), the court stated: "We specifically hold the term 'financial exigency' as used in the contract of employment herein may be limited to financial exigency in a department or college. It is not restricted to one existing in the institutions as a whole."

The *Krotkoff* v. *Goucher College* case clearly establishes that an institution does not have to liquidate capital and assets before a financial exigency may be declared. However, an institution may not remove thirteen tenured faculty and at the same time hire twelve new faculty, as was done in the *American Association of University Professors* v. *Bloomfield College* case. Enrollment declines can be used to justify the existence of a financial exigency and the removal of a specific faculty (*Brenna* v. *Southern Colorado State College*, 1978; *Krotkoff* v. *Goucher College*, 1978).

Identifying Appropriate Decision Makers. The second issue is to identify those authorized to develop and implement the criteria for layoff as a result of a financial exigency. Clearly, the board of trustees or the equivalent body has the authority to make these decisions as stated in every case reviewed. It is also apparent from the case law that the board may delegate that authority to the president (*Johnson* v. *Board of Regents of the University of Wisconsin System*, 1974; *Klein* v. *The Board of Higher Education of the City of New York*, 1977). However, general guidelines developed by the board within which the president or others should arrive at layoff decisions were present in most of the cases reviewed. Department heads or deans are also qualified to select those to be laid off within the general guidelines (*Brenna* v. *Southern Colorado State College*, 1978; *Krotkoff* v. *Goucher College*, 1978). In most of the cases, the layoff recommendations were also supported by recommendations of faculty study committees organized to evaluate and recommend appropriate action (for example, *American Association of University Professors* v. *Bloomfield College*, 1974; *Brenna* v. *Southern Colorado State College*, 1978; *Krotkoff* v. *Goucher College*, 1978).

Defining Appropriate Criteria. The third issue is the criteria appropriate in selecting faculty for layoff because of financial exigency. The cases indicate that non-tenured faculty should, in most cases, be selected first and that tenured faculty must be given the opportunity to fill vacant positions for which they are qualified. Certainly, as noted above, declining enrollment can be used to select programs where faculty cuts may be made. However, the courts also say that the administration or board has discretionary power to decide where cuts will be made when a financial exigency exists, as long as their decisions are not arbitrary and capricious (for example, *Johnson* v. *Board of Regents of the University of Wisconsin System*, 1975).

The case law also indicates that seniority rules need not be used. In the *Krotkoff* v. *Goucher College* case, a tenured faculty member with more seniority was selected for removal over a younger faculty member because the younger faculty member had the qualifications to meet the curricular needs of the college more effectively. In *Brenna* v. *Southern Colorado State College,* a non-tenured faculty member of a two-faculty department was retained instead of the tenured faculty member. The reason given was that the non-tenured faculty member gave the department more flexibility in making teaching assignments because the tenured faculty member had stated that he was not qualified to teach courses other than those he was currently teaching.

The use of published criteria, however, such as competency as a teacher or researcher, would implicate the faculty member's property interest under the Fourteenth Amendment. This would mandate due process requirements of a hearing prior to layoff as indicated in the *Perry* v. *Sindermann* and *Board of Regents* v. *Roth* cases, since the ability to get employment elsewhere may be in jeopardy, requiring greater precaution in preventing unfair or unjustified damage to one's reputation. The due process requirement would be less for a financial exigency (where no reference to a person's competency was part of the reason for dismissal) because it does not affect future employment opportunities or deprive the person of his reputation. It should be noted that choosing faculty on the basis of the individual's qualifications to perform certain tasks is appropriate and within the administrative discretionary decision.

Clarifying Due Process Procedures. Since the tenured faculty member at a public institution who is laid off because of financial exigency is being denied a property interest (the person's job), the Fourteenth Amendment is implicated. The due process requirements under financial exigency as mandated by courts have been less than those mandated for a faculty member removed for cause (for example, incompetence or moral turpitude). In *Johnson* v. *Board of Regents of the University of Wisconsin System,* the court outlined the specific requirements necessary to meet the tenured faculty member's rights to due process. The court states the following procedures (1974, 377 F. Supp. 240):

1. Furnish each plaintiff with a reasonably adequate written statement of the basis for the initial decision to lay off.
2. Furnish each plaintiff with a reasonably adequate description of the manner in which the initial decision had been arrived at.
3. Make a reasonably adequate disclosure to each plaintiff of the information and data upon which decision makers had relied.
4. Provide each plaintiff the opportunity to respond.

The University of Wisconsin unit chancellors selected faculty to serve on a reconsideration committee. The committee was to review the faculty member's response and might (but was not required to) agree to meet with the faculty member. This meeting was not to be an adversarial situation, or a situation in which the university must prove its position, but rather a time for the faculty to show why the university rationale should not be followed or to correct erroneous information. The court stated that the reconsideration committee should determine whether sufficient evidence supported the layoff decision and ensure that the procedures spelled out by the system had been followed. The court also ruled that the unit chancellor could make the initial layoff decisions, appoint the faculty to serve on the reconsideration committee, and also make the final layoff decision without violating the due process rights of the faculty member. In support of these procedures, the court cited *Arnett* v. *Kennedy,* a 1974 Supreme Court case in which these procedures were applied to a layoff where permanence was attached to employment. Other cases have followed these standards; thus this Wisconsin case suggests an appropriate due process in the dismissal of tenured faculty when financial exigencies exist (see: *Brenna* v. *Southern Colorado State College,* 1978; *Bignall* v. *North Idaho College,* 1976; *Klein* v. *The Board of Higher Education of the City of New York,* 1977; *Krotkoff* v. *Goucher College,* 1978).

Describing the Liability Issue. In a case entitled *Grany* v. *Board of Regents of the University of Wisconsin System,* a group of terminated faculty of the University of Wisconsin System brought a liability suit against the Regents. The court ruled that the doctrine of sovereign immunity prevented state officials, acting in the normal role of their office, from being sued. However, damage claims could be brought (in Wisconsin) against the individual for "negligent performance of ministerial duties." The court ruled that the dismissals were within the officials' discretion, were conducted under procedures that did not deny faculty protections owed them, and were not arbitrary dismissals for personal reasons. There were no other allegations of "malicious, willful, or intentional misconduct by board members" and, therefore, the suit was dismissed (1979, 286 W.W.2d 138).

Personal liability claims could arise in financial exigency cases where a faculty member could show that the decision was arbitrary, that the decision was made for reasons other than those stated, or that procedural rights were denied. A claim could also be supported if it could be shown that the faculty member's constitutional rights at a public institution had been violated. The Supreme Court in *Wood* v. *Strickland,* 1975, held that a civil claim for damages would be possible if a public official were to deny an individual his rights under the Constitution. Ignorance of those rights was no defense against a liability claim. Data collected and evaluated by institutional research offices will help in making fair and equitable decisions and in preventing the appearance of an arbitrary and capricious process.

Implications for the Institutional Researcher

The tenure contract, financial exigency, and due process procedures have significant implications for the data gathering and planning tasks of the institutional researcher in periods of retrenchment.

First, as curator of the institution's data, and as a member of the campus planning team, he or she can heighten the institution's awareness of the need for careful planning and proper procedures to respond to financial exigency.

Second, if procedures for layoff include provisions to protect the quality of programs, instead of simple seniority-generated methods, those procedures must be clarified. The institution needs discretion to make decisions about offering programs and employing faculty while maintaining academic standards. Administrative discretion in a layoff decision is supported by the case law, but it would be eliminated if seniority-based procedures were specified or normally followed.

Third, if the institution has not already done so, it would seem appropriate to develop a data base on how departments are interrelated to each other in terms of course enrollments as described in Johnstone's chapter (in this volume). These data will help a faculty curriculum committee and the administration to identify whether programs or departments should be eliminated or scaled down to a service function and the effects these cuts will have on the course enrollment in other departments.

Fourth, enrollment projections may help determine future curricular and faculty levels. If so, the projection methodology should be documented in as easily understood a manner as possible. Documentation of projected enrollment changes and their effect upon interrelated departments may allay charges of arbitrary or capricious action.

Fifth, the institutional researcher should maintain records on faculty work load data or ensure that such records are kept by other offices. Current and previous work experiences can be related to future program needs and thus be legally used in the layoff decision.

Finally, data presented in court are more effective if they are collected as part of the normal course of business and have been collected during each of the academic years under consideration. All of this information can become part of the "reasonably adequate information and data" for the layoff decision.

The above information plus the data proving financial exigency may best be prepared by the institutional researcher. He or she would have access to the necessary sources, be trained to present complex data in a form that is understandable and useful, and have the responsibility of supplying the "reconsideration committee" or similar group with appropriate information for evaluating layoff decisions. Legal counsel should be consulted to evaluate the propriety of the data in light of litigation needs and due process requirements.

Because all the above information would come under the scrutiny of a court in a contested layoff, it should be properly compiled, accurately stated, and free from bias or appearance of bias against a particular faculty or program. Thus, the institutional researcher is a key person in the retrenchment process. Contested cases may be won or lost based on the quality of the data and analysis presented to support a layoff decision.

This chapter is intended to provide the institutional researcher with an understanding of the legal issues involved in financial exigencies. It should help the reader to identify specific questions and areas of concern in consulting with legal counsel. This is not the definitive work on financial exigencies, and much could be written on any of the issues contained in this chapter. Each institution is strongly urged to obtain legal counsel not only for this reason but also because the laws governing both contract and liability vary from state to state.

References

American Association of University Professors. "On Institutional Problems Resulting from Financial Exigencies: Some Operating Guidelines." *AAUP Bulletin*, 1974, *60*, 270.
American Association of University Professors v. *Bloomfield College*, 129 N.J. Super 249, 322 A.2d 846 (1974).
Arnett v. *Kennedy*, 416 U.S. 134 (1974).
Bignall v. *North Idaho College*, 538 F.2d 243 (9th Cir. 1976).
Black's Law Dictionary. St. Paul, Minn.: West Publishing, 1980.
Board of Regents v. *Roth*, 408 U.S. 564 (1972).
Brenna v. *Southern Colorado State College*, 589 F.2d 475 (10th Cir. 1978).
Brown, R. C. "Tenure Rights in Contractual and Constitutional Context." *Journal of Law and Education*, 1977, *6* (3), 279-318.
Browzin v. *Catholic University*, 527 F.2d 843 (D.C. Cir. 1975).
Duerr, C. A. "Termination of Tenured Faculty." Unpublished outline prepared

for the Mid-Winter CLE Workshop of NACUA by Jackson, Lamb, and Duerr, 61 North Huron Street, Ypsilanti, Mich., March 1, 1980.

"Financial Exigency and Reduction—In Force." *The School Law Newsletter*, 1978, 7 (6), 287-293.

Grany v. Board of Regents of the University of Wisconsin System, 286 W.W.2d, 138 (1979).

Holloway, J. P. "Termination of Faculty Due to Financial Exigency." *The JOURNAL of the College & University Personnel Association* (Washington, D.C.), Spring 1980, *31* (1).

Iowa Law Review. "Financial Exigency as Cause for Termination of Tenured Faculty Members in Private Post-Secondary Educational Institutions." *Iowa Law Review*, 1976, *62* (2), 481–521.

Johnson v. Board of Regents of the University of Wisconsin System, 377 F. Supp. 227 (W.D.) Wis. 1974) Aff'd. 510 F.2d (7th Cir. 1975).

Kaplin, W. *The Law of Higher Education: Legal Implications of Administrative Decision Making.* San Francisco: Jossey-Bass, 1978.

Klein v. The Board of Higher Education of the City of New York, 434 F. Supp. 1113 (S.D.N.Y. 1977).

Krotkoff v. Goucher College, 585 F.2d 675 (4th Cir. 1978).

Perry v. Sindermann, 408 U.S. 593 (1972).

Rolles v. Civil Service Commission, 512 F.2d 1327 (D.C. Cir. 1975).

Scheuer v. Creighton University, 260 N.W.2d 595 (Neb. 1977).

Wood v. Strickland, 420 U.S. 308 (1975).

Robert M. Hendrickson is an associate professor in the Center for the Study of Higher Education at the University of Virginia. He recently completed an ERIC monograph on law and higher education.

*An institution facing faculty retrenchment often
overlooks political considerations that may
greatly affect the retrenchment process.*

What if the Faculty Member to Be Laid Off Is the Governor's Brother?

Colleen Dolan-Greene

Beware of making a faculty layoff decision in a political vacuum. It is not enough to project faculty employment needs, to decide whether all units will suffer or only one, to analyze the budgetary and indirect implications, and to consider legal aspects (see Dougherty, Johnstone, and Hendrickson chapters, respectively, in this volume). All that effort can be wasted if the political realities of retrenchment are ignored or overlooked. An institutional research director who is an active participant in the planning for faculty reductions should alert the institution to this fact and could play a key role in predicting political realities. Two questions should be considered: (1) What are the distinguishing characteristics of the institution and the departments affected by the retrenchment? and (2) Why is the retrenchment occurring? This chapter will review the implications of both questions and highlight some of the experiences of institutions that have already implemented reductions. In addition, it will outline the policies that institutional research needs to develop concerning the release of data during a retrenchment.

The Personality of the University

Every university has a fairly unique personality that is the result of a combination of characteristics. Though personalities of different universities can be similar, no two are identical, and the distinctions will affect the retrenchment action. The institutional research director and other administrators who are knowledgeable about their institution should carefully review what they know and how the characteristics of the personality will affect any contemplated action. There are six sets of somewhat contrasting characteristics that can make a difference for an institution facing retrenchment: (1) institutional support—public or private, (2) faculty governance—strong versus weak, (3) faculty unionization—unionized or non-unionized, (4) executive leadership—strong versus weak, (5) academic reputation—excellent or mediocre, and (6) history of layoffs—initial versus repeated retrenchment. In addition, size contributes to a university's personality and can affect the politics of retrenchment. Each of these characteristics will be examined in order to highlight the type of political complication it can cause.

Institutional Support. The tongue-in-cheek title of this chapter suggests one aspect of the complications of institutional support. A state supported university could come under severe political pressure if the governor's brother was on the layoff list. It also may not be prudent to lay off the sister of the senator who heads the appropriation committee, but there may be occasions when an institution wants to do just that. For example, if the layoffs are necessitated by reductions in state appropriations, then one of the quickest ways to get the message to the state legislature about the real impact of such a budget may be to target a program for reduction which, even if it does not include the sibling of an important politician, is a favored program of a politician. That tactic should be used with caution and is mentioned only to illustrate an extreme. In actual practice it is more likely that the planning process will identify a program for retrenchment, and no one will have considered the political connections of the program. That was the case in 1977 when it was proposed that the speech and hearing service program of the Medical School be closed at the University of Michigan, based on evaluation of eroding academic quality coupled with the university's fiscal constraints.

Somehow it was overlooked that two of the members of the Board of Regents were also serving on the advisory board of the special speech therapy camp run by that department. It was quickly apparent that, even if the department were to disappear, the summer camp would continue.

Independent universities face a different set of possible political reactions when faced with retrenchment. Obviously, they also have boards that may be connected with a program or faculty member affected by retrenchment. More important for a private college's survival is the reaction that its major contributors may have. A benefactor who is vocal about his support and his interest in a particular program will probably be given deference when reductions are considered, even though a program is rarely supported entirely by one contributor. A greater need will be for someone (and why not the institutional research director?) to discover the not-so-obvious connections and examine some possibly unexpected outcomes. For instance, there is an immediate impact on fund raising when retrenchment occurs. Fund raising is hurt because people don't want to be associated with a loser. Just as Chrysler's automobile sales fell drastically when its government loan guarantees were being negotiated, rumors of retrenchment can slow the inflow of development funds, and actual retrenchment can dry it up completely. In turn, this could trigger a new round of retrenchment.

The internal politics of an institution should be considered in relation to financial support. Because tuition is the source of most revenue at independent institutions, the impact on enrollment of any program reduction should be considered carefully. A downward spiral can be caused even by reductions in nonacademic programs. As mundane a step as a deferral of maintenance, carried to the point that the campus becomes seedy-looking, can quickly affect enrollment prospects. Independent institutions can take solace from the observations of one author commenting on the descent from the "golden years" in higher education. Cheit (1973, p. v) stated that "private institutions seem to have adjusted more quickly and more adequately than public institutions."

Faculty Governance. There is a tradition in higher education, or at least a legend, that it is the faculty who allows the administration to govern an institution. As Mayhew stated (1979, p. 226), "that mandate can be removed by both overt and covert means." If there is the practice of a strong faculty governance structure, then the revocation of the mandate may occur at least partially in the open forum of the faculty senate. The mechanics of retrenchment at many universities require the involvement of the faculty senate or at least a subcommittee of that body. The possibility of open discussion of details should be remembered when the decision is made to cut back programs or personnel. The administrators should not optimistically assume that decisions will not be questioned. Indeed, the opposite is more likely. It is not uncommon for a faculty to censure the president during a time of retrenchment. The impact of faculty discussion and action following a retrenchment announcement will be further explored in the second and third section of this chapter.

It is extremely unpleasant for a faculty body to have to consider which individuals should be laid off. As Mix noted (1978, p. 21), "the faculty want responsibility for formulating criteria for decision making, but they do not want to implement the decisions they themselves make, for example, which faculty will be dismissed." Traditional governance structures do not provide for such decisions (Mortimer and Tierney, 1979, p. 53). Any institution facing retrenchment should consider whether the faculty governance structure can withstand the trauma of being involved in the deliberations necessary to implement a reduction. It may not be practical to avoid action solely out of concern for the impact on governance, but the long range impact of action on even an effective governance structure should not be ignored. If the structure is weak at the time of retrenchment, it may be overcome by the political impact caused by the reduction.

Faculty Unionization. The bridge from an unorganized faculty to one represented by a union has frequently been provided by retrenchment. This is a political reality that any administration approaching such action should consider. It has been observed by Mayhew (1979, p. 226) that if the faculty is not consulted prior to action, they will probably unionize. He cites the University of San Francisco as an example. This was also the case at the University of Detroit, as will be described later.

Prior to announcing a retrenchment, it may be possible to alter the faculty's perception that union protection is needed. One key can be to provide due process. Any discussion of awarding or removing tenure will necessarily include consideration of due process. An institution may not be prepared to go as far as Rehmus suggested (1968, p. 12) in providing due process and establishing a grievance procedure that ends in neutral, binding arbitration. However, most institutions already have a grievance procedure established to handle tenure or discrimination complaints, and the administration should review it and decide if it is appropriate or can be modified to handle problems that result from retrenchment. As Rehmus noted, "the keystone of the grievance process is the possibility of review of administrative decisions by qualified and independent neutrals" (p. 12). If the institution does not provide due process, the faculty may seek it in a court of law. In addition, if there is a perception that due process is lacking, it is probable that the American Association of University Professors (AAUP) will review the action after the fact.

In 1977, 1978, and 1979 the AAUP added to its censure list institutions that had implemented retrenchments without using "generally accepted academic standards" ("Developments Relating...," 1980, p. 222). The institutional research director and other administrators will have to judge what political impact AAUP censure would have on their campus. Because the AAUP is now considered to be a faculty union, the reaction to censure might be minimized. However, censure can create public relations problems for an institution, and the institutional research director should help the institution plan for this.

Campuses that already have a faculty union have other political realities to face when retrenchment is contemplated. The faculty union may be a partner in the decision. Unions have been successful in becoming involved in the retrenchment process. As Lozier has observed (1977, p. 244), "Specific provisions for faculty involvement in the development and implementation of retrenchment procedures were present in seventeen of the twenty-one four-year [institutions'] contracts, but in only thirteen of the thirty-three contracts for two-year institutions." He noted further that faculty involvement through a union, rather than through a faculty senate, is more common at two-year institutions.

Before the collective bargaining agreement is negotiated, the institution will need to decide what it feels is an acceptable role for the faculty union in retrenchment decision making. Then, in negotiations, an attempt can be made to write this into the contract.

In the abstract, it may be difficult to perceive that the involvement of the union can "at least for the short run, be antithetical to the economic well-being of the institution" (Mayhew, 1979, p. 65). However, any retrenchment decision must deal with the probability that the faculty union will be primarily concerned with protecting the membership and not in the quality of programs or the finances of the institution. The union will press its demands during the process of retrenchment, and if unsuccessful in providing job security, it will probably challenge both the process and notices of layoff issued to individuals through the grievance procedure. In planning for retrenchment, the administration should be aware that the political realities of the effort will linger long after action is taken. This is particularly true when the faculty union challenges the action through the grievance procedure or by funding a legal challenge of the process.

Executive Leadership. It has been observed by Mayhew (1979, p. 30) that "the majority of serious institutional pathologies stem from administrative failure." This should be remembered when trying to gauge the possible political reactions to retrenchment. It has already been noted that the faculty may respond by attempting to censure the president. If that occurs, what will be the board's reaction? Will it support the president and the administration, or will it use the censure vote to justify the dismissal of the president? If there are administrative deficiencies, how are they correctable? "Rectifying administrative deficiency may not solve serious institutional problems, but not doing so will ensure continuation of serious difficulty" (Mayhew, p. 63).

A common tactic of a faculty faced with program reductions and layoffs is to challenge the size of the administration. A simple but dangerous response to this tactic is to reduce the number of administrators or add to their duties. Retrenchment is a time when serious challenges face an institution's administrators and they find themselves burdened with more details and responsibilities. If there is a surplus of administrators or types of administrative programs, it is advisable to cut back and thereby be better prepared for the faculty's questions. If there is not a surplus, the administration should be prepared to demonstrate the necessity for the number and types of administrators.

A strong executive officer will prepare the institution for the possibility—or in the eighties, the likelihood—of retrenchment. Careful planning may allow the institution to reduce the number of programs through attrition without actually having to lay off faculty. Yet there is a psychological impact on even the strongest executive who has to administer decline (Mayhew, 1979, p. 64). Institutions will probably find themselves in the presidential search process more frequently in the 1980s and 1990s with all the political ramifications that such searches produce. To retain executives with management and leadership skills, an institution that can foresee decline, and even faculty layoffs, should make every effort to provide support for the chief executive and other administrative officers who must manage decline.

Academic Reputation. A strong academic reputation can be an advantage in two ways to an institution that faces retrenchment. First, if the university has long been identified with excellence, it is easier to justify those reductions designed to preserve quality education. The goals of maintaining and strengthening a few high quality programs will be politically more acceptable than merely deciding which mediocre lamb is first to be sacrificed for the sake of a mediocre flock. Preferably, such an institution will have an established practice of making qualitative judgments in faculty personnel decisions. This can provide it with its second advantage, the strong support argument that deciding who is to be laid off should be based not only on seniority but also on the strengths of the faculty members. Such an argument can be attractive, but it can also be political dynamite. As was noted earlier, it is not easy for faculty to participate in any decision regarding who is to go. Tenure decisions have long been based on confidential review of colleagues, but recent court challenges have questioned this. It is doubtful that confidentiality can be maintained when layoff decisions are being made at a time of an extremely limited market for faculty members.

An institution with a strong academic reputation can also be at a disadvantage as a result of that reputation. Though it is doubtful that anyone will articulate it so bluntly, it may be tempting to allow quality to diminish throughout an institution rather than face the harsh reality of eliminating a program. The institutional research director should be sensitive to this and bold enough to warn the institution not to take the easy road.

An institution that has been improving the quality of certain programs can have a political uproar on campus if it proposes a program reduction or elimination. That was the case at Temple University, according to Scully (1979, p. 4). When reductions were proposed, the layoff list included many visible, respected faculty members who had been recently hired and brought to Temple to help upgrade the quality of graduate programs and advanced research.

History of Layoffs. An institution that has never experienced a faculty retrenchment is liable to react in shocked disbelief to the word that a reduction is being planned. This will be true although the higher education press has carried many stories about the decline expected in the 1980s. If a programmatic reduction is announced, the students can usually be counted on to rally in support of their majors. Student papers will question the wisdom of the administration's decision, just as they question most decisions. The faculty who are affected will argue valiantly in support of themselves and the essential nature of their program. Many alternatives will be suggested, but they may be highly impractical. The institutional research director and other administrators should consider what skeletons may be in the institutional closet prior to any announcement. Does the university own a golf course that it intends to maintain although faculty will be dismissed? Is there a palatial mansion full of antiques, valuable paintings, and gold plumbing fixtures occupying the most prominent hill on campus? Has someone just awarded the university a grant to begin a major research project that will require the hiring of talented researchers and faculty in a new program area while other programs are being eliminated and faculty with different backgrounds are being laid off? It is much better to consider the existence of such non-instructional costs, prior to the announcement of a layoff, so that truthful and appropriate responses can be prepared to the questions that will be asked by students and faculty.

Administrators at institutions that have experienced retrenchment in the past should avoid a callous attitude toward the prospect of another layoff. It is possible that the faculty will be better prepared to react to any new plans for reduction because they have been through it before. The political climate may be changed because a different program has been identified for reduction or elimination. An administration that has gone through the exercise of carefully predicting the political consequences of a faculty retrenchment should be at an advantage because of the experience gained the first time. An institution should be careful not to lose that advantage by not following all the steps again.

Institutional Size. At a small institution, everyone tends to know, or at least know of, everyone else. This can be a tremendous advantage in fostering a strong sense of community, but it can be a disadvantage when the college experiences a loss. In the past this has been most frequently demonstrated when a small campus suffers the death of a member of the community. Faculty retrenchment brings another type of loss. Since the faculty is small, the impact will be tremendous. The relief experienced by the faculty members who do not receive a layoff notice will be quickly followed by grief for colleagues who did. Such action can split the strong sense of community that existed between the faculty and administration. Suddenly, the faculty will perceive that the administration is on the other side, and it may take years for the split to heal, if it does at all.

Large institutions have the depth of faculties and programs to insulate them from this aspect of retrenchment. The loss to any individual who is laid off is as great, and the impact on the colleagues in the department will still be there. But in larger institutions, it is less likely that the entire campus will be affected. In addition, large research institutions have had experience in dealing with program reductions even before the decline in student enrollments. Research projects and special grants come and go. New ones frequently demand faculty researchers who have different skills and specialities from those demanded by the previous grants. However, it will still be a drastic shock when retrenchments occur in teaching units. The institutional research director and other administrators should reflect on the differences and be prepared for them.

The Reasons for the Retrenchment

A careful review of the personality of an institution and the characteristics that contribute to that personality will be beneficial to the institutional research director and other administrators who face the probability of retrenchment. The first part of this chapter has highlighted some of the political effects of those characteristics. Through a review of institutional experiences in program reduction, this section will outline various reasons why retrenchment may be necessary and discuss how those reasons can also dictate political reactions. Learning from experiences at other institutions, institutional research directors should be able to minimize the political problems of retrenchment by predicting what may happen.

Program Elimination. The first retrenchment case to be considered occurred in 1976-77 at the University of Michigan's Department of Population Planning (DPP) in the School of Public Health (SPH). The institution is state supported, though this particular retrenchment decision was partially necessitated by a reduction in outside support. There is a well-established faculty governance structure at both the school and university levels. Although many state institutions in Michigan are unionized, there has not been enough support for a faculty union at the University of Michigan to call for a union election. Each school and college at the university takes pride in its autonomy, which focuses executive leadership at the dean's level. The SPH dean had been appointed in July 1974. The vice president for academic affairs is the chief budget officer and therefore plays a significant role in any retrenchment decision. The academic reputation of the university is very strong. Richard D. Mandell (1977), in ranking American colleges and universities, discusses twenty-five great institutions, one of which is the University of Michigan. As is true with major research institutions, it was not unusual to have retrenchments of research areas supported by outside funding, but it was not common to have a reduction or elimination of an academic area. At the time this retrenchment recommendation was made, the university developed a policy to handle such situations and the School of Public Health was used to test the process. It is helpful to examine this retrenchment action in light of the history of the school. It was established in 1941 and the specialty of population planning was established in 1965. The program grew; in 1971, it was recommended that a separate department of population planning be established. The Board of Regents approved this recommendation in September 1971.

On July 9, 1974, the Executive Committee of the School of Public Health approved a procedure for the periodic review of all departments and programs. Detailed procedures that outlined the steps in the review went into effect in October 1975. The Department of Population Planning (DPP) was one of the initial three departments selected for review. As a result of that review, the executive committee recommended that DPP be eliminated, so the details of the procedure are important. Every five years a review was to focus on a specific program and the resources required to support it. The review was to assess the progress during the preceeding five years and to examine goals in light of the school's and the department's priorities. Existing problems were to be identified and future plans and requirements reviewed. In addition, there was to be a review of the commitments made by the university to the chairperson, with an evaluation of how well they had been fulfilled.

In accordance with this procedure, a population planning review committee was established in the fall of 1975. It was composed of five faculty members and two students from the School of Public Health, and two outside consultants. The review procedure required that, while reviewing the department, a decision would be made either to reappoint the department chairperson or to allow a relinquishing of the chair without onus.

On July 20, 1976, the review committee presented its finding to the executive committee which consisted of the dean and members of the faculty appointed by the board on the president's recommendation. Its purpose, according to the regent's bylaws, was to act as the executive officer for the school. In addition to assisting with administrative functions, it was also charged with investigating and formulating educational and instructional policies for consideration by the faculty, and acting for the faculty in matters of budget, promotion, and appointments.

The first drafts of the outside consultant's report and the review committee's report were shared with the population planning faculty and department chairperson. In September 1976, both the faculty and chairperson were given separate opportunities to discuss the reports with the executive committee.

Both reports focused on academic weaknesses in DPP. The teaching load was low in both credit hours taught by individual faculty members and credit hour production for the entire department. Despite the light teaching load, research productivity was also low. Faculty members were seen as primarily operating as external consultants to outside agencies. This was seen as a further weakening of the department because the consulting activity was done either individually or in small groups and did not contribute to the reputation of the department.

While the executive committee was reviewing the reports and discussing them with faculty, students, and the chairperson, the dean was faced with financial problems for the school. It was expected that by 1978 major institutional funding from the Ford Foundation and the Agency for International Development (AID) would end. Both had provided major assistance to DPP. In September, the dean and his staff presented to the vice-president for academic affairs and the central administration the cumulative effects of federal funding losses, which dated from 1969. The estimated annual shortfall was expected to be $900,000 by 1978-79. The DPP funding loss from Ford and AID would raise the shortfall to over $1 million per year.

An additional problem presented itself when the DPP chairperson resigned. (The chairperson had been with the program since it was established in 1965.) The executive committee and the dean considered what was needed to recruit a new chairperson. It was difficult for them to imagine that a strong academic leader could be attracted to DPP without the commitment of funding to support new faculty positions, but current circumstances made it hard to justify additions. Given the projected reduction in funding for the entire school, growth in DPP could only occur by imposing severe restrictions on the operations of the other eight departments.

On February 2, 1977, the dean sent the "Final Recommendation Arising from Review of DPP" to the SPH faculty and the review committee. It recommended the dissolution of DPP, effective July 1978. The executive committee could not justify placing DPP as the highest priority in SPH (which would be necessary to make up DPP's funding loss). The recommendation promised to honor contractual obligations to tenured faculty by reassigning them to other departments whose programs most closely matched the training and interests of individual faculty. To minimize professional disruption, it was also promised that maximum possible notice of termination would be given to faculty members without tenure and to other staff. This recommendation was forwarded to the Board of Regents for its February 17, 1977 meeting.

The political realities of the recommendation quickly became apparent. On February 4, the DPP faculty wrote an open letter to all SPH faculty, challenging the executive committee's recommendation on the basis that the school's governing faculty had not been consulted. The DPP faculty proposed a special meeting of the governing faculty on February 14. The dean responded by scheduling a special meeting on February 21, since the February 17 Board of Regents meeting would only be for initial discussion of the recommendation. In his response, the dean pointed out the broad, faculty-wide input that had been sought and received throughout the review process.

The faculty of DPP simultaneously sought support outside the university by addressing a letter to all other schools of public health and programs dealing with population planning. In the letter, they asked anyone with comments on the proposed action or DPP's quality to write the regents in care of the president, with copies sent to individual regents at their home addresses.

During the second week in February, the vice-president for academic affairs proposed procedures for "Discontinuance of Academic Programs." The regents were to review the procedure at their February 17 meeting; final guidelines would be approved by the board in March. The proposed process had three steps. First, an independent faculty peer group would review the proposed action. Second, the Office of the Vice President for Academic Affairs would review and decide on the recommendation, giving particular attention to university-wide implications. Finally, the board would review and act on the recommendation.

The vice-president decided to use the DPP case to test the procedure. Representatives from his office were assigned to review the DPP recommendation. They were to meet with the faculty during February.

The interim procedure stated that the criteria for eliminating a program ought to place the greatest emphasis on the quality and viability of the program. The quality issue was the primary one for the DPP faculty. The challenge to the executive committee's action was based on the inconsistency between their recommendation and the findings of outside consultants and the review committee regarding quality. The faculty's communication focused on the quality issue and their right to participate in any decision to eliminate a department.

Political reaction to the recommendation to discontinue DPP came primarily from three sources: off-campus persons, students, and faculty. The off-campus response was both national and international. Reviewing the files, it seems that as many letters came from outside the United States as within. This is a reflection of the makeup of the student body in DPP. In the fall of 1976, nearly one third of the students were from outside the United States. Interestingly, very few of the letters came from residents of Michigan, yet the regents are elected by the people of the state. It is possible that, had there been a stronger showing of support from Michigan residents, the final decision might have been different.

The student response came from recognized channels of representation. The Public Health Student Association (PHSA) protested the manner in which the decision was made. Their objection was that the executive committee had reached its decision without having open meetings and notifying students and faculty. Prior to the February 17 regents meeting, the PHSA demanded that the issue of DPP be reopened and the department allowed to present its case. The Asian Public Health Student Association, affiliated with the PHSA, joined in the procedural objections. However, the Asian PHSA primarily objected to the dissolution of DPP based on the substantive issue that population planning is an essential element of public health of particular importance in the third world. Both of these objections were directed to the regents prior to the February 17 meeting. The quality issue was used in a challenge sent to the dean on February 28. The Public Health Student Association took issue with statements that appeared in the press about the quality of DPP. They felt that such comments had damaged their career prospects. It was demanded that the dean formally and publicly apologize to them.

The faculty's response was formally solicited as part of the application of the interim procedures for the discontinuance of academic programs, when the Office of Academic Affairs conducted an independent review of the recommendation to phase out DPP. Part of that review included a series of meetings held with the faculty. The faculty also reacted when the SPH Governing Faculty passed a resolution on February 21 charging the dean and executive committee to reconsider the question of terminating DPP and requesting that that curriculum committee, augmented by the department review committee, examine the role of DPP.

Faculty response outside SPH and DPP was apparent when the University of Michigan chapter of the American Association of University Professors (AAUP) passed a resolution on the discontinuance of DPP. It found that academic due process had been violated because the dean and executive committee had not sought faculty participation in the decision and had not given notice that the departmental review could result in program termination. In addition, the chapter charged that no justification had been provided to show financial exigency and the need to discontinue DPP. The vice-president for academic affairs was urged to take no action until the faculty of SPH decided on the termination of DPP.

In response to the governing faculty's resolution, a report was issued on March 16 by the curriculum committee augmented by the departmental review committee. On that same date, the executive committee passed a motion as a result of their reconsideration of the discontinuance of DPP. Both the report and motion recommended that an identifiable research and teaching presence be continued by the establishment of an interdepartmental Center for Population Planning with a director and an executive board. The report was unanimously adopted by the school faculty.

In April 1977, the Board of Regents approved the recommendation that DPP be dissolved and a Center of Population Planning be established. Looking back three years later, the dean stated that he would still make the same recommendation despite the months of turmoil. However, he feels that the public and political nature of the process will discourage other deans from closing a department under this procedure. The dean feels that the pocess should be less public and that the public nature of the process is a reflection of the management style of the vice-president under whom it developed. The vice-president believed that every issue could be carefully reasoned. If a proposal is made to close another department, it will be interesting to see if the dean's perceptions are correct. Perhaps the past three years (the process hasn't been used again) bear testimony to the dean's observations and suggest that other deans are now developing ways, in effect, to discontinue a department without using the procedure.

Reallocation of Positions. The second retrenchment case to be considered occurred in the 1975-76 academic year at Oakland University. Oakland is located on the former Wilson estate, given to the state of Michigan for a branch of Michigan State University (MSU). In 1970, the university became independent of MSU, with its own board of trustees appointed by the governor, and its own president. That same year, the faculty decided to unionize and affiliated with the American Association of University Professors. The two events are related. Oakland was originally envisioned as an elite liberal arts institution. A high quality faculty was recruited with that goal in mind. When it became apparent that the institution was developing into a regional university serving a portion of the state's population, the faculty became disillusioned. The faculty unionization is at least partially the result of the disillusionment. The negotiations for the first collective bargaining agreement broke down at the beginning of the fall term in 1971, and Oakland has the dubious distinction of being the first four-year college or university to be closed by a faculty strike.

The person appointed to be Oakland's first president was one of the faculty members recruited to start the university. His original peers were involved in organizing the faculty union during his first year in office. As a result of collective bargaining, the role of the university (faculty) senate was challenged, and each year's negotiations resulted in at least slight changes in the type of issues that came before the senate.

The faculty retrenchment at Oakland took place under the provisions of the collective bargaining agreement. The agreement that brought a settlement of the 1971 strike did not cover retrenchment. However, it did contain a gross gauge of faculty work load measured by a student-faculty ratio. The ratio concept had been used by the state of Michigan in the appropriation process, and it was incorporated into the collective bargaining agreement under the pressure of the strike. The 1974-75 faculty agreement was the first one to contain provisions for layoff. The language of the agreement was somewhat abstract because neither side had any layoff experience or expectation that there would be a need for a layoff. The agreement gave the university the right to institute a layoff when the number of positions allocated to a unit exceeded the need in that unit. There was also provision for an expedited layoff with very short notice periods if there was a drastic reduction in the number of students.

Much to everyone's surprise, the regular layoff provisions that contained notices similar to those used in the tenure procedure were used in 1974-75. The university found itself with over-staffing in Modern Languages because the general educational requirements had changed and students were no longer required to take languages. Because five layoff notices were issued, the faculty union filed a grievance.

During the bargaining for the 1975-76 agreement, the layoff provisions were modified. Under that contract, when there was a decline in the student-faculty ratio, a regular layoff could occur with notice periods similar to those used in the tenure process. When there was a shift in student interest and demand, a position-shift layoff could occur. In that case, for every layoff in one unit, an additional position had to be added to another. The expedited layoff with its shortened notice periods had become a concern for the national AAUP. As a result, the Oakland AAUP proposed that, rather than an expedited layoff, the contract allow an automatic salary reduction when there was a drastic reduction in the number of students. Such a provision was included in the contract.

In October 1975, although the grievance over the 1974-75 layoff notices was still active, the director of institutional research prepared enrollment projections that became the basis for the 1976 position-shift layoffs. The projections focused on the expected enrollment by unit for 1977-78. That year was used because, if a layoff was announced in January 1976, it would be the end of the 1976-77 academic year before any layoff could be implemented.

On January 14, 1976, two sets of notices were issued in accordance with the faculty agreement. The first went to units that were losing a total of twenty positions as a result of the position-shift layoff. They were advised that the tenured full-time faculty within the affected department had sixty days to make a recommendation about the order of layoff. The second set of notices went to units that were gaining positions.

The AAUP was officially notified of the position-shift layoffs the day after the units were notified. The contract provided forty-five days for the union to comment on the proposed reallocations. Layoffs were planned in seven academic units. Two units would be virtually eliminated. One was the Academy of Dramatic Arts, which was a two-year, non-degree program to train professional actors. The other was the Classics Department. Program offerings would be affected in the other five units. All communications from the university to the AAUP, the departments, and the faculty expressed the strong hope that normal faculty turnover before the spring of 1977 would make it possible to avoid actual layoffs.

The president of the Oakland AAUP asked that the university senate use the existing constitutional process to find alternatives to the layoffs. In effect, the AAUP was recognizing that the faculty governance structure could continue to play a separate role in the university despite the existence of a faculty union. The steering committee of the senate responded by asking the Academic Budget and Planning Committee to study the fiscal circumstances surrounding the administrative judgments leading to the decision. The Academic Policy Committee was to study the academic implications of the matter. Both committees were encouraged to develop alternative solutions to the problems that the position-shift layoffs attempted to solve. The two committees decided to join forces and tackle the problem in the two weeks they were given to comment. Six subcommittees were established on the following topics: budget alternatives, academic effects on the university and alternatives, position alternatives, possibilities of alternatives in enrollment trends, tenure implications and alternatives, and constitutional implications and alternatives.

The joint committee reported on alternatives to the proposed position-shift layoffs on February 13, 1976. The committees had one motion, three resolutions, and seven recommendations. Their motion supported the elimination of the Academy of Dramatic Arts unless adequate private endowment could be acquired to support it. The body of the report stated that this would not reduce but rather improve academic quality, because the training of professional actors could be replaced by a liberal arts degree administered by Speech Communications.

The first resolution recommended that the College of Arts and Sciences reconsider the proposed position-shift layoffs. If the new recommendations were to suspend a degree program, a major, or an academic unit, then it was recommended that the senate have the opportunity for full debate and legislative action.

Tenure was the topic of the second resolution. The body of the report recognized that the meaning of tenure had changed as a result of deleting the 1940 AAUP statement on academic freedom and tenure and substituting layoff provisions. Instead of using the economic security concept of the 1940 statement, the Oakland layoff procedure was changed to focus on seniority within a department. This was an obvious problem for the faculty on the senate committees. The second resolution recommended to the president that, wherever possible, tenured faculty members capable of useful instruction would not be laid off by a position-shift layoff.

The third resolution was a recognition of the need to plan for the future. The body of the report repeatedly identified organizational problems or questions, such as the need for a process to reevaluate and reconstitute programs and the impact new programs or general education requirements have on enrollment. It was recognized that, at a time of steady state enrollment, a consensus was needed about the configuration of the university.

By the end of March, most of the units had submitted a proposed order of layoffs to the university. Oakland was unable to agree to the order proposed for one department, and in accordance with the faculty agreement, the contested order was submitted to the Faculty Reemployment and Promotion Committee (FRPC) on March 30. That same day, layoff notices were sent to faculty members in units where there was agreement on the order of layoffs. Since the grievance filed as a result of the 1974-75 layoffs in Modern Languages was still awaiting the arbitrator's decision, faculty in that department received notices as part of the position-shift layoffs in 1975-76. Many of these Modern Language faculty members were then confused about their status, having been notified once of a layoff (effective at the end of the 1975-76 academic year) that was later appealed, and then having been notified again under a separate layoff decision. Clarifying telegrams and letters were sent to the faculty members. The controversy was settled on May 1 when the arbitrator's opinion was received. It upheld the layoffs and the faculty members were so informed.

It should be noted that the university cancelled layoff notices to departments on three different occasions when natural attrition took care of over-staffing. This was consistent with the university's original statements on January 15, when the position-shift layoff process began. It was also consistent with the university senate resolution about tenured faculty.

The FRPC responded with a proposed order of layoff for the contested department, which Oakland found acceptable. The second group of layoff letters was sent on April 29.

In the interim, the AAUP filed a grievance stating that the proposed layoffs did not take into account the impact of faculty attrition on the staffing level in three departments. This grievance was settled by extended discussion on July 27, 1976, and layoff notices were left in effect as a result.

The layoffs became effective May 1, 1977. Two other protests were filed by the AAUP after that date. On July 21, the AAUP wrote the provost and objected to laying off faculty when departments with new positions had not been successful in filling them. This matter was dropped by the AAUP in August following a discussion of the situation with the provost.

On October 25, 1977, the chairperson of the Classics Department filed a grievance protesting Oakland's alleged intention to have certain courses in the classics curriculum taught while classics faculty members were laid off. In response, Oakland denied it had any such plans. However, the university also asserted its right to follow such a course if it so desired, under the provisions of the collective bargaining agreement. Following the first answer by Oakland, the grievance was not carried forward by the AAUP.

It is obvious from reviewing the history of the position-shift layoff that the faculty union and the university senate had an effect on both the process and the outcome of the 1975-76 position-shift layoffs at Oakland. Since that time, there have been no other faculty layoffs. To some extent, this is due to changes in the contractual language about the student-faculty ratio, which make initiating a layoff more difficult. However, since enrollment has been increasing, there has been no need for a regular layoff. More importantly, the university is now using better management techniques and taking advantage of regular faculty turnover to avoid a situation like the 1975-76 year, when drastic action was needed to redistribute faculty positions.

Financial Exigency. The third case of layoffs occurred at the University of Detroit in December 1975, as a result of financial exigency being declared by the Board of Trustees. This university is an independent institution founded by the Jesuits in 1876. It has three campuses. The original campus is now the site of the Law School and the evening business administration program. It is located downtown just across from the Renaissance Center, which is a symbol of the city's revitalization. The Dental School has a separate campus a little over a mile east of the Law School. The main campus is in the northwest section of the city. The university had a very weak faculty governance system in 1975. The university's president has by tradition been a member of the Jesuit order. At the time of the 1975 terminations, the president had been in office since 1966 and had seen the university through the end of the turbulent 1960s and the racial unrest that had occurred in the city and on the campus.

The university's small endowment contributed to a long history of financial difficulties. Enrollment began to decline in the early 1970s, and by the 1974-75 academic year, a group of faculty had therefore been issued terminal contracts. Most of these notices had been rescinded when regular turnover reduced the size of the faculty. Another method that the university had used to reduce or prevent a deficit was to eliminate vice-presidential positions. This led to a compounding of problems because there was no longer proper oversight and sound financial procedures were not established or enforced.

This deficiency had been recognized by the Board of Trustees. On July 1, 1975, a new Vice-President for Business and Finance took office. It was his challenge to normalize the budget process and help establish a sound financial base.

The 1975-76 academic year was opened on an optimistic note by the president in his remarks to the faculty. However, the new vice-president quickly discovered that the university faced serious problems. Unless corrective measures were taken, a deficit of at least $2 million was projected for 1977-78.

The president appointed a special Budget Planning Committee, chaired by the vice-president, to develop a plan to avert a major deficit. That plan was approved by the Board of Trustees on December 23, 1975. In approving the plan, the board declared that a condition of financial exigency existed and the elimination of forty faculty positions was necessary. The board also took steps to assure the long-term stability of the university by approving the appointment of an executive vice-president (EVP). The president was to concentrate on fund raising while the EVP would be responsible for the administration of the university. The vice-president became EVP and was authorized to recruit a vice-president for academic affairs, a vice-president for student affairs, and a replacement for himself, that is, a vice-president for business and finance.

Following the board's decision, the Christmas holidays of faculty, chairpersons, and deans in the two affected colleges were devoted to identifying which faculty members were to be terminated. The dean of faculties consulted with the dean of the affected colleges, the university's legal counsel, and the Academic Affairs Council of the University Senate, in order to develop criteria to be used in selecting faculty. Weighted criteria were developed (which totaled 100%):

Programmatic Need	50%
Length of Service	20%
Scholarship	15%
Teaching Effectiveness	10%
Terminal Degree	5%

Every department was instructed to develop a clear statement of program goals and to use that to apply the weighted criteria. By December 29, the two affected deans had to submit a list of faculty members to be terminated, along with a statement of the procedures used and a list of programs to be continued.

Forty faculty members received their termination notices by January 1; twenty-nine of them were tenured. Faculty were terminated in accordance with administrative procedures that provided for one year's salary in lieu of notice. The affected faculty members were immediately relieved of all teaching and other responsibilities, and fringe benefit coverage stopped.

The challenges to the university's action began even before the individuals were notified, and the political ramifications continue today. Prior to the individual notices, a group of faculty had petitioned the National Labor Relations Board (NLRB) for an election to determine whether there would be formal collective bargaining. This would be the third election at the university. In late 1973, during the last vote on collective bargaining, the choice had been to join no union, the campus chapter of the AAUP, or an affiliate of the National Education Association (NEA). A runoff election was necessary and a majority of the university's faculty voted for no union. By late 1975, the AAUP/NEA rivalry had ended and, in what was claimed at the time to be a first, a coalition between an NEA and an AAUP chapter petitioned to represent the faculty.

This coalition made plans to seek a court order to block the faculty terminations even before individuals were notified. Though the terminations were not successfully blocked, the court challenge resulted in a legal case that has not been completely settled at the time of writing this chapter.

The faculty coalition adopted the name "The University of Detroit Professors' Union" (UDPU). During the spring of 1976, it was obvious to the university administration that the UDPU would be successful in the NLRB election, so a Director of University Personnel was recruited who had experience in faculty collective bargaining. The faculty union was a reality before the director assumed office on May 10, 1976.

Negotiations for the first collective bargaining agreement began in November 1976, and were concluded by March 1977. The primary issue for the UDPU was economic security. The final agreement contained an article on layoff that stipulated the procedure to be followed in the case of a layoff. However, in a separate letter of agreement, the university promised not to issue any layoff notices to any tenured faculty during the term of the contract, which expired August 15, 1979. In addition, the faculty members who had been terminated January 1, 1976, were to be treated as if they were on layoff status until March 11, 1979, with full recall rights to any positions that would become available in their departments.

The coalition that had formed the UDPU was not formally recognized by the AAUP or NEA. But in October 1976, the UDPU formally affiliated with the Michigan Educational Association (MEA)/NEA. This too had an impact on the politics of this retrenchment. At the time the first faculty contract was settled, the UDPU announced that the MEA/NEA had agreed to provide legal support to faculty members protesting the 1976 terminations. As was mentioned earlier, this case is still in litigation, although the majority of the plaintiffs have reached individual settlements as a result of diligent efforts of university and union representatives.

In the summer of 1979, when the second faculty contract was being negotiated, the issue of job security was still a key to the settlement. At that time, the university was in the process of recruiting a new president, which caused a great deal of uncertainty. The UDPU once again demanded a moratorium on the retrenchment of tenured faculty. When a new president was selected, he had to decide even before assuming office whether this was acceptable to him. He agreed to the moratorium for the period of a two-year contract because financial forecasting could reasonably look that far into the future. It will be interesting to see how both sides approach the politics of retrenchment in the summer of 1981, when a new collective bargaining agreement will be negotiated.

The Role of Institutional Research

The challenge for any director of institutional research when the institution is considering retrenchment is how to face what Mayhew has called (1979, p. 130) "a sort of academic Murphy's law. . . . That every conceivable difficulty will in fact present itself." An intelligent reflection on the personality of the institution and the reasons for the retrenchment highlight some possible difficulties. The director should be prepared with two items before a layoff decision is made. First, accurate and reliable data should be available as a basis for the decision that the university administration must make. Second, a policy must be established which defines who is eligible to receive the data.

Reliable Data. The importance of accurate information is obvious from the cases presented. The reviews that led to the program elimination at the University of Michigan criticized the Department of Population Planning because the credit-hour load of the faculty was much lighter than in other departments. This was challenged by DPP, and information was circulated to all faculty members in the school contesting this claim. The dean eventually had to respond in writing to that challenge.

At Oakland, one of the reasons for layoffs is directly tied to a mathematical calculation of the student-faculty ratio. Even if a labor agreement does not require it, most institutions will examine the student-faculty ratio before instituting a layoff. The ratio is most valuable when historical and interdepartmental comparisons were available.

The University of Detroit case is an example of the importance of financial information that is sometimes maintained by institutional researchers. As Hendrickson demonstrates in another chapter in this volume, universities have had to justify the claim of financial exigency in a court of law. It has not been easy, and there is a guarantee that claims of financial exigency will be carefully examined when used to justify what is a traumatic experience for the affected faculty members. At a minimum, on most campuses a committee of the faculty senate will review this information.

Access to Data. Before a retrenchment decision is announced, institutional researchers should develop a policy that clearly defines who will have access to information. This policy should be approved by the institution's president, since it may be challenged in the heat of the political reaction to the decision.

Full access should be provided to the academic deans, administrative officers, and board members who are responsible for making the decision. There are five other groups that might seek access.

The first is the affected faculty. When a department is asked to identify someone for layoff, the faculty will want to see the data that justify the decision. The types of information to be released and the manner in which they are provided need to be determined in advance. From a human relations perspective, the most difficult challenge will be to respond to faculty members who are laid off. The termination decisions at the University of Detroit were challenged by many individual faculty members. A committee of the university senate reviewed the procedure used in making the decision and made a stunning discovery: A simple mathematical error when the weighted criteria were applied resulted in the wrong faculty member being terminated. Based on similar errors, the committee recommended (and the board approved) reinstatement of five faculty members.

The second group is the faculty senate. In all three cases the senate played an important role in responding to the politics of retrenchment. It is usually best to provide as much infomation as possible to this group. However, this administrative decision may be influenced by the role and strength of the institution's faculty senate.

The faculty union is the third group. The collective bargaining agreement may define what information must be supplied to the union. If it does not, there is a strong possibility the union will demand access to certain information. The university's legal counsel and labor relations staff should be consulted when the policy is developed concerning the union's access to information.

The fourth group is comprised of students. At the University of Michigan, students majoring in population planning objected to statements made by the administration. Although their challenges were not quantitatively based, they were factual.

The news media make up the fifth group. The public relations staff probably has a policy about the release of information to the news media. That policy should be reviewed by the institutional research director and other administrators when retrenchment is imminent. The public relations staff can assist institutional research in another way by making the data understandable. A matrix presentation may be fine for deans who review the same data every semester, but data may be more understandable when presented in a different fashion to the general public, the news media, students, and faculty.

Conclusion

Lozier stated (1977, p. 25) that "the diplomacy with which retrenchment is handled will determine to a significant degree the amount of turmoil through which an institution and its faculty will have to go." Diplomacy can be achieved by predicting the political realities that may occur during retrenchment. This can be done by first identifying the distinguishing characteristics of the institution and the department affected and, second, reviewing why the retrenchment is occurring. Neglected but foreseeable political realities should not prevent the institution from taking necessary action.

References

Cheit, E. R. *The New Depression in Higher Education—Two Years Later.* Berkeley, Calif.: Carnegie Foundation for the Advancement of Teaching, 1973.
"Developments Relating to Censure by the Association." *ACADEME,* Bulletin of the American Association of University Professors, 1980, *66,* 213-224.
Lozier, G. G. "Negotiating Retrenchment Provisions." In G. W. Angell, E. P. Kelly, Jr., and Associates, *Handbook of Faculty Bargaining: Asserting Administrative Leadership for Institutional Progress by Preparing for Bargaining, Negotiating and Administering Contracts, and Improving the Bargaining Process.* San Francisco: Jossey-Bass, 1977.
Mayhew, L. B. *Surviving the Eighties: Strategies and Procedures for Solving Fiscal and Enrollment Problems.* San Francisco: Jossey-Bass, 1979.
Mix, M. C. "Tenure and Termination in Financial Exigency." Higher Education Research Report No. 3. Washington, D.C.: ERIC, 1978.
Mortimer, K. R., and Tierney, M. L. "The Three 'R's' of the Eighties: Reduction, Reallocation and Retrenchment." Higher Education Research Report No. 4. Washington, D.C.: AAHE-ERIC, 1979.
Rehmus, C. M. "Collective Bargaining and the Market for Academic Personnel." *The Quarterly Review of Economics and Business,* Autumn 1968, pp. 7-13.
Scully, M. B. "Cutting Back at Temple: The Hard Lesson of Retrenchment." *Chronicle of Higher Education,* October 15, 1979, pp. 3-5.

Colleen Dolan-Greene is the personnel administrator for the personnel service center for all schools, colleges, institutes, and libraries at the University of Michigan. She first faced the politics of faculty retrenchment as labor relations manager at Oakland University in Rochester, Michigan. Next she experienced the aftermath of retrenchment when she became personnel director at the University of Detroit four months after forty faculty members were terminated because of financial exigency.

*The issues of faculty reduction will require
increasing sophistication in planning and
budgeting. The institutional research professional
must play a central role.*

Budgeting for Retrenchment

Wm. A. Johnstone

As we enter the 1980s, there are many scenarios for American higher education, ranging from pessimistic enrollment declines and extensive closings of institutions to enrollment increases with new clientele and extended research and public service roles. It is clear, nevertheless, that many institutions will be adversely affected by declining enrollments. Faculty cutbacks will be inevitable at many institutions during the coming decade.

The Recent Perspective

Many states have already gained some experience in dealing with these issues. In Montana, for example, although the state university system headcount increased 5.8 percent during the last decade, variations among the six individual institutions ranged from a gain of 40.1 percent to a loss of 20.9 percent. Full-time equivalent (FTE) enrollment changes ranged from a gain of 31.1 percent to a loss of 42.9 percent. Four of the six units lost both headcount and FTE enrollments.

This declining enrollment, coupled with a legislatively mandated higher student-teacher ratio, dictated a reduction at one university of about sixty faculty in 1978 and another fifteen in 1980—an overall decrease of more than 15 percent. Although statewide enrollment has been relatively stable, enrollments have shifted at individual campuses, both in total amounts and by disciplines within those totals. These shifts, combined with other factors (for example, failure of appropriations to keep pace with inflation) created financial emergencies on some campuses, led to faculty layoffs, and prompted a statewide study of the budgeting process for higher education.

With enrollment declining in four of the six units of the system, the rapid expansion of graduate and undergraduate programs ended. Program moratoria were ordered by the regents, new role and scope statements were prepared, central academic staff were added, and more rigorous review procedures were developed both for existing and proposed degree programs. At one university, a thorough self-study of all graduate programs recommended phasing out twenty programs or options. Programs in liberal arts, authorized in the 1960s at the smaller units, were eliminated. The changes in Montana during the last ten years have led both to program elimination and faculty layoffs, as well as changing governance patterns, budgets inadequate in concept and amount, and changing patterns of support.

And so it was in the nation. The problems discussed in this sourcebook can no longer be seriously viewed as potential; they have arrived. However, the fifty state systems of public higher education differ in their programs, procedures, problems, and plans. Within these systems, campuses differ greatly. Within campuses, operational units differ. Thus, standard solutions to the problems of enrollment decline and financial pressure cannot be offered with confidence. The one clear implication that is applicable to all institutions is that careful, detailed thought will be essential in the budgeting process as never before. The issues to review in deciding how best to use scarce resources are extremely complicated. The budget planner will have to examine the heart of his assumptions regarding both the purposes of his institution and the methods to be used in meeting them. This effort to assign honest priorities demands analysis that is defensible, not only to others in the institution but to external observers as well.

The role of supplying information and interpretation to state coordinating and governing boards is demanding. Even more difficult is the task of providing that support to legislative analysts and executive budget specialists, who often now have anonymous but major impacts on university operations through staff work for legislative committees and the governor. These external participants must not be overlooked even in the most preliminary efforts to develop budgetary strategies for dealing with scarcity. Thorough analysis, properly prepared and documented, strengthens budgetary requests to the state, although final effectiveness is also mitigated by political and fiscal constraints. Good analysis is essential. It is evidence of effective management and helps develop confidence among reviewing agencies, among appropriation committees, and within the college or university itself. Integrity and validity are keys. Trust is obtained after much time, effort, and care; it can be lost with one careless presentation.

To handle contemporary budget issues competently, access to an information system will be a prerequisite. Much of the concern in this decade will be on the allocation of resources, which will be the deciding point on faculty retrenchment and program redirection. Even with the most capable management assisted by the finest technical analysis, facing these problems will be a painful process.

Budget Modeling for the Coming Decade

With financial pressure so clearly a matter of future concern, most budgeting models of the past twenty years will be inadequate to meet the demands of the 1980s. There is more than ever before a need for long range financial planning based on realistic academic plans.

Improved budgeting models and methods are needed and are being developed. At present, a combination of existing models is often used, since each has shortcomings. Incremental budgeting works from an inflexible base. The formula approach provides a basis for cost comparisons, but it routinizes decision-making and may be based on institutional comparisons that are not well founded. Zero-based budgeting (ZBB) and Program Planning and Budgeting System (PPBS) are models that encourage rational decision making, but they are time consuming. Objectives, strategies, and tactics (OST), however, may provide the systematic, long-range planning so vital in this decade and can allow involvement by those concerned at the operational level. In OST, objectives are broadly defined quantitative statements of intentions and purposes; strategies are long-term general plans of action aimed at the achievement of objectives; and tactics are short-term plans supporting a strategy. An excellent and complete description of OST is provided in the *1973 Annual Report* of the Southern Methodist University Institute of Technology (pp. 23-39).

Crisis management cannot properly meet the challenges of the 1980s. If retrenchment is necessary, it cannot be achieved properly on a "crash" basis. The linkage of planning and budgeting will be required. Enthusiasm for such systems has waned in recent years, but the difficult financial decisions facing higher education demand the use of more "scientific" methods of budgeting. OST is worthy of consideration as one method, but there are many others.

The Role of Institutional Research

When faculty reduction is demanded by the legislature or dictated by financial conditions, careful analysis based on sound data is required. As Dougherty notes in another chapter of this volume, an across-the-institution percentage faculty reduction is the simplest response, but it is shortsighted. Similarly, it may not be in the best interests of the institution or the society it serves simply to dismiss untenured faculty when cutbacks are required. For the internal allocation of scarce resources, zero-based approaches to budgeting offer great potential for rational program decisions. Several important things can be accomplished by such a review: all activities of the institution are examined at the most discrete level rather than at the department or college level, alternate methods of achieving the objective are considered, priorities are developed, and the most thorough program review is accomplished.

In this development of detailed and sophisticated budgetary planning, increased reliance on the institutional research professional is likely to develop. Technical analysis and effective political action are necessary components of budgeting; timely information and institutional data expertise are essential. As decisions become more difficult and complex, the use of this sort of analysis will increase.

Of course, there is a limit to the role of the institutional researcher. Institutional research provides background information for study and evaluation but does not provide decisions. Models, formulas, systems, and methods do not give answers on values or interests, but they should assist in making better decisions. And despite implications of data, other factors such as human, social, or political interests may prevail. Nevertheless, the institutional researcher will become a central member of the budget team. As Caruthers and Orwig (1979, p. 61) have noted: "Several roles are necessary in the budget process: advocates, cutters, analysts, decision-makers, providers and expenders ... less visible though increasingly important are institutional analysts."

Institutional researchers may serve as catalysts, even as goaders in the basic need for articulation of concise goals for the institution and its operating units. In the rapid growth period of the past twenty years, researchers helped to define an expanding role. Now they may well be involved in defining a more effective role. Occasionally this will mean program elimination or curtailment as well as the development of new areas of service.

While incremental budgeting required the institutional researcher to analyze the relative growth of different components in campus programs and budgets, newer and more demanding systems will require more sophisticated data and techniques to address the more difficult "Where shall we cut?" planning questions.

Getting Started—Useful Background Approaches

Many techniques will be developed by institutional researchers to address questions of retrenchment, and a range of factors will affect the approach adopted by an institution. The nature of the approach is likely to be affected by the nature of existing—rather than preferred—available data. The formats for data vary according to custom, state reporting requirements, and the extent to which computer-assisted information systems have been developed. Although formats and procedures may evolve into standard approaches, a variety of approaches currently exists. The remainder of this discussion is devoted to a review of sample data formats and methods of analysis that may be used to plan for problems of faculty reduction and reallocation. It is not too soon to begin initial efforts, and even fairly simple data analyses will provide insight.

There are four basic sources of useful information that are likely to exist on most campuses. Review and discussion (with wide participation, if possible) of these data will provide a strong background for planning future campus operations. Briefly, the data are: instructional production by department, faculty profiles, cost variations by program and instructional level, and financing of support activities.

Instructional Production. A first step is to determine, even in the most basic way, the nature and extent of campus instructional activity. Several sources of these data are possible. Many campuses maintain detailed reports on departmental operations. For example, for the past three years, a department profile has been maintained at Montana State University (MSU). Data are presented for a four-year period and are consolidated by college or school and summarized for the university. This year, department heads—who previously reviewed the data before release—have been asked to add their comments to the final report. Initially, information to be included was determined at a meeting of academic deans and key central administrators. Although fiscal policies dictated the operational units for reporting, some further programmatic breakdowns are also cited. An outline of contents follows:

Program—*Instruction*
I. Students
  1. Majors by level
  2. Degrees conferred
II. Production (student credit hours)
  1. Fiscal year by level
  2. Summer quarter only by level
  3. Autumn quarter only by level
III. Faculty
  1. Full-time equivalents by rank
  2. Computed staffing pattern
  3. Average salary by rank
  4. FTE faculty on grant and contract
IV. Financial (by personnel, operations, capital)
  1. July 1 budget plan (unrestricted)
  2. Expenditures for fiscal year (unrestricted)
  3. Expenditures (restricted) grant and contract

Program—*Research*
V. Organized Research
  1. Agricultural Experiment Station
    a. July 1 budget (personnel, operation, capital)
    b. Expenditures for fiscal year (personnel, operations, capital)
    c. Personnel (faculty FTE, GRA FTE)
  2. Other Organized Research Units
VI. Sponsored Research (grant and contract)
  1. Expenditures (personnel, operation, capital)
  2. Personnel (professional FTE, GRA FTE)

The structure of the ongoing report is developed in conjunction with the intended users of the data. The addition of short comments from each department head is encouraged along with a preliminary review of the data. Experience has shown that the department profiles constitute a convenient source of popular data and have been used for many more purposes than originally imagined.

An added report that has merit is illustrated by Table 1, which was also developed for each department.

Table 1. Suggested Measures of Instructional Production and Efficiency

Type of Instruction (NCHEMS)	Lower Division Credits Taught	Lower Division Student Credit Hours	Lower Division Average Class Size	Upper Division Credits Taught	Upper Division Student Credit Hours	Upper Division Average Class Size	Graduate Credits Taught	Graduate Student Credit Hours	Graduate Average Class Size
Lecture	1,270.0	78,875	57.4	1,064.0	28,747	27.0	246.0	1,804	7.3
Lab/Studio	661.0	13,942	21.1	568.0	7,099	12.5	53.0	491	9.3
Rec/Discuss	365.0	8,381	23.0	211.0	3,378	16.0	30.0	325	10.8
Seminar	17.0	475	27.9	85.0	1,148	13.5	22.0	135	6.1
Prog. Instr.	1.0	22	22.0	—	—	—	—	—	—
Subtotal	2,314.0	95,695	41.4	1,928.0	40,372	20.9	351.0	2,755	7.9
Indep. Study[a]	9.7	175	—	173.5	3,112	—	45.0	450	—
Thesis[b]	—	—	—	22.0	220	—	177.4	887	—
Tutorial[c]	42.0	210	—	11.6	58	—	1.0	5	—
Total	2,365.7	96,080	—	2,135.1	43,762	—	574.4	4,097	—

[a]Credit Adjustment: undergraduate level— 18 SCH = 1 credit
                    graduate level— 10 SCH = 1 credit
[b]Credit Adjustment: undergraduate level— 10 SCH = 1 credit
                    graduate level— 5 SCH = 1 credit
[c]Credit Adjustment: all levels— 5 SCH = 1 credit

Some institutions maintain similar data in on-line accessible computer files from which they can prepare custom reports (for special topics), listing only the most relevant portions of the total data and presenting the information in any of several formats.

Each of these data sources is a valuable component in creating a realistic picture of existing circumstances and recent trends. Without such a beginning, reasoned analysis of how best to use instructional resources would be most difficult.

Faculty Profiles. Faculty employment should also be directly addressed. Many administrators are so occupied with present problems that it is difficult to plan for those of the future. Faculty employment may well be one of the most critical future problems with severe budget implications. The institutional researcher can assist in bringing these questions into focus and active consideration. First, however, an analysis of current faculty employment and a projection of a future faculty profile will be required. To approach this question, one could:

1. Project enrollment and full-time equivalent (FTE) instructional faculty based on current staffing patterns. (In one application of this basic exercise, a possible 25 percent decrease in faculty over the next ten years was projected.)

2. Develop a table of ages and tenure status of current faculty. (At this institution, 57 percent were tenured, and only 18.6 percent of these were fifty-five or older; the median age was in the 40-44 year age group.)

3. Estimate retirements, resignations, and tenured positions based on present policy and experiences in recent years.

4. Consolidate this into a profile for the 1980s.

The results are guaranteed to gain the attention—if not the acceptance—of the faculty. For the management, it could provide incentive for long-range strategic planning of personnel policies.

Cost Variations by Program and Instructional Level. Academic departments normally account for at least 60-65 percent of the total instructional operating budget (excluding research, public service, and scholarships). Therefore, the method used in determining the budgetary needs of these credit-producing organizational units is most important.

If there is to be equity or fairness, neither simplistic student-faculty ratios nor a fixed amount per student will suffice. All programs do not have the same cost, whether in a university or a community college. To illustrate this, an academic cost per Student

Credit Hour (SCH) chart used in budget development in Texas has been reduced here for easier comparisons to indices based on undergraduate liberal arts equalling 1.00. There are other models that would provide different cost figures for lower division and upper division production, but the important point of relative cost differences can be illustrated by Table 2. For example, undergraduate nursing instruction evidently requires (in that state system) 3.23 times as many resources per unit as liberal arts at the same level. Doctoral work in engineering was judged to be 19.86 times as expensive as undergraduate work in the liberal arts.

Other cost-factor tables have been developed in many other states (New Jersey, Colorado, and New Mexico, for example) and vary in appearance by showing discipline-specific costs per student, student-faculty ratios, or productivity ratios for faculty members. The benefit of using rigid, detailed ratios in statewide budgeting is questionable. Some states find that formula budgets using these factors are quite beneficial, while other states report very unfavorable experiences. Most would agree that such data provide a basis for valuable discussion, if not actual budget determination; such data should be of particular value at the campus level.

The impact of recognizing these cost differences in budgeting can be illustrated by assuming an institutional loss of production of

Table 2. Sample Indices[a] of Unit Costs of Instruction by Program and by Level

Program	Under-graduate	Masters	Special Professional	Doctoral
Liberal Arts	1.00	2.92	—	11.08
Science	1.44	5.91	—	19.86
Fine Arts	2.26	5.50	—	19.95
Teacher Education	1.06	2.46	—	9.40
Agriculture	1.64	5.10	—	18.25
Engineering	2.31	6.02	—	19.86
Home Economics	1.50	3.30	—	9.84
Law	—	—	2.41	—
Social Science	1.58	4.72	—	10.72
Library Science	1.21	3.31	—	11.08
Veterinary Medicine	—	—	6.62	22.98
Nursing	3.23	6.09	—	22.06
Pharmacy	3.17	5.56	—	19.95
Business Admin.	1.19	3.51	—	14.18
Optometry	—	—	4.01	19.86

[a]Based on Liberal Arts undergraduate SCH = 1.00

100 units of undergraduate liberal arts and a gain of twenty units of doctoral engineering. If an extremely simple per-student-appropriation were used, the institution would receive eighty fewer units of resources. However, if cost indices listed in Table 2 were applied, the institution would receive an *increase* of 377.2 resource units. Both of the above calculations are examples of formula budgeting in which the weighting factors have a great impact on budgeting.

A loss of enrollment should not always result in a budget reduction for departmental instructional costs. The type of program, level of instruction, and existing costs must be considered along with enrollment to determine an equitable resource allocation. The institutional researcher will be called upon to assess the impact of alternate retrenchment plans. A strong understanding of budgetary implications will be needed.

A related and valuable background tool in preparing for reduction analysis is the induced course load matrix (ICLM). Developed by the National Center for Higher Education Management Systems (NCHEMS), ICLM has proved to be useful when program elimination has been proposed.

Reactions to proposed institutional cutbacks range from disbelief and the feeling of impending catastrophe in departments with small or declining enrollments to apathy in other campus departments to concern by administrators as a loss of enrollment is translated into a loss in the budget.

Campus reactions to externally suggested cuts in specific departments are interesting. Last year, an acting commissioner proposed phasing out the elementary education program at MSU. The general effects would have included:

1. The loss of 350 full-time students, which would have caused a campus budgetary loss of nearly $1 million yearly under the current simple budget formula.

2. The elimination of 18.4 FTE faculty positions (based on the present student/faculty staffing plan mandated by the legislature).

3. The loss of a viable state program that has been an important source of elementary teachers for the public schools of Montana and surrounding states.

The reaction of the elementary education department was immediate and pronounced. The reaction within many other departments was a passive relief that the cut was being applied to some other unit. At this point, the administration requested an ICLM-style report from the office of institutional research and the registrar. The use of the ICLM computer program provided detailed information on the specific impact of the reduced enrollment, including changes to courses taught (contributed) by the elementary education department and taken by students from other fields, and courses taken (consumed) by elementary education majors in other departments. The contribution report stated that, while 60.8 percent of this department's student credit-hour production was for its own major, 9.8 percent was for students majoring in other departments in the College of Education and 20.2 percent for students in other colleges or schools. Thus, a significant number of non-education majors would be deprived of courses currently taught by elementary education. The consumption report stated that, contrary to the belief of some critics, elementary education majors do take most of their academic work in other departments. Among principal departments providing instruction were mathematics (9.3 percent of the total), library science-educational foundations (6.8 percent), earth science (6.8 percent), health and physical education (6.4 percent), home economics (5.9 percent), music (5.6 percent), art (5.1 percent), speech (4.8 percent), and English (4.2 percent). The closure of the elementary education programs would therefore reduce enrollment (and budgets) in these other departments.

Departments are interrelated; the impact of a program elimination on other departments should be known before decisions are made. This basic use of institutional research data should not be underestimated.

Financing of Support Activities. Enrollment declines are not the only cause of faculty reductions. Gathering and understanding the impact of non-instructional financial data is an important element in planning for reduction. The thrust of this volume is on general planning for faculty reduction. However, if inadequate funds are available for support activities, management is faced with a decision of curtailment of services or retrenchment in the instructional programs to provide for increased utility and other support costs.

Halstead's Higher Education Price Index (HEPI) in Table 3 indicates that cost increases in the university operations vary widely (1978, p. 19).

If the library is expected to maintain minimally the current rate of purchases of books and periodicals (and that is below faculty expectations) while operating at least as many hours as before (and students clamor for longer hours), there is a problem when its capital

Table 3. Halstead's Higher Education Price Index (HEPI)

Year	Professional Salaries	Fringe Benefits	Books and Periodicals	Utilities	H.E.P.I.
1967	100.0	100.0	100.0	100.0	100.0
1971	127.5	162.0	144.8	114.6	128.6
1975	153.6	241.0	219.5	202.9	166.2
1978	177.9	324.3	286.4	292.5	201.3
Yearly Average Increase 1967-1978	7.1%	20.4%	16.9%	17.5%	9.2%

budget is increased 5 percent while book and periodical costs are now increasing by nearly 20 percent each year. A library budget is, in part, a function of enrollment, but it is also dependent upon the type of institution, the programs offered, and changes in the cost of books and periodicals.

Rapidly rising utility costs and expenses in other support areas present campus managers with the difficult decision of cutting programs to maintain campus operations. Institutional research studies on projected utility and other costs will also be required. Knowledge of financial conditions in these support areas is necessary in calculating future resources available for faculty employment.

Computer Modeling

A basic understanding and exploration of the uses and potential of computer modeling for financial planning is an important step in getting started. During the past decade, many computer models, such as RRPM and CAMPUS, have been developed to project enrollments and calculate needed budgets. Such models fail to consider the quality of programs, long-range strategies, and political considerations. They are often not used to the extent originally envisioned but do have the ability to change variables easily—enrollment, acceptable class size, and so forth—and to obtain a revised estimate of faculty needed for the programs offered. As such, they may provide a useful guide or initial reference point for determining budgets under different budget assumptions.

To illustrate this sort of use, in one model (Bennett, 1972), faculty time requirements are developed for preparation, contact, paper grading, and student conferences. Adjustments are made if class enrollment is less than twenty or over forty. No preparation time is allowed for the second section of a lecture course. Time is also allocated for supervision of independent study; for example, it is assumed that dissertation supervision requires one hour each week per credit per student. Minimum class sizes are established for "countable" credits. However, any course specifically required for a degree is counted regardless of enrollment. Policy on sectioning of classes is considered. Time is allowed for advising, based on the number of departmental majors, and for departmental administration, based on FTE faculty in the department.

The number of faculty needed, as indicated by a model, can then be compared to current budget allocations as another measure of equity. A repeated warning is that no one measure, of itself, should be thought to be the answer. A variety of measures coupled with management judgment are required. Such systems can be very valuable not only to examine complex relationships but also to avoid very basic errors. For example, a serious problem has developed in state financing at several institutions (and will be a problem at many more in this decade): Many enrollment-driven budgets assume a direct and absolute relationship between faculty requirements and student enrollment whereby a 20 percent loss of enrollment mandates a 20 percent reduction in faculty. If programs and levels of quality are to be maintained, this is not valid. Bennett's budget model just described was used to evaluate 1979-80 actual enrollment data and to compute the corresponding number of required FTE faculty. Using the same assumptions of minimum class sizes and required courses, but with only an 80 percent enrollment level, the computer model calculated that 87.1 percent as many faculty would be needed. The theoretical number of faculty required varied by the level of instruction: 84.9 percent at the lower division level, 87.5 percent at the upper division, and 87.8 percent at the graduate level. The slightly lower percentage at the lower division level corresponds to a greater number of sections of each course and resulting staff flexibility. At the graduate level, only a single section of a required course is usually taught, preventing any staff reduction unless the program that requires the course is altered or dropped. Thus, the computer model is one way to determine possible staff reductions and to demonstrate to funding agencies that, if all programs are to be continued, a given drop in enrollment usually does not allow the same drop in required faculty.

Such budget models offer an excellent tool for projecting the impact of various enrollment and budget changes upon other segments of the institution. These computer models are not likely to produce final budget decisions, but they can be an effective tool of institutional researchers, providing reference points and suggesting the impact of various strategies to cope with faculty reduction. It is important that the institutional research professional be prepared to provide the needed expertise in their use.

Conclusion

During the next few years, institutional research offices will be charged with greater responsibility in the budgeting process. More sophisticated analysis will be required as management faces the problems of declining enrollment; certainly the major issue of faculty retrenchment demands the highest quality of management coupled with the skills of capable technical analysts. The budget process is often where decisions on these problems are finally made.

There are continual challenges for higher education budgeting. Caruthers and Orwig (1979, pp. 4-5) suggest that it is essential that the institutional researcher learn to:

- Understand the fixed and variable nature of resource allocation in higher education.
- Understand the organizational and decision-making process in budgeting.
- Understand the impact of entering new markets.
- Integrate academic planning and budget activities.
- Adapt budgeting techniques to the unique needs of colleges and universities.
- Measure financial implications of collective bargaining.
- Improve enrollment forecasting.

Two other approaches should be considered. First, it is evident that new program requests, such as those of the 1960s, will not satisfy state policy makers in the 1980s. Too often new programs were presented with no financial considerations; courses and faculty were said to be already available, and student demand and societal needs were deemed self-evident. The costs were being paid from growth and an enrollment-driven budget. New methods should be developed for more carefully assessing the financial implications of program changes. Second, as considerable control of public institutions apparently passes from the campus to the capitol, there is an increasing need to develop liaison with state officials to assist in reaching proper conclusions based on the best data that can be supplied. More accurate and informative data, improved methods of analysis, and better budgeting formats to present program needs fairly and concisely should be developed jointly by campus and capitol staff. If this is coupled with the best judgment of highly qualified persons at both levels, schools and society will be well served.

Change is a fact of institutional life. Without change there would be stagnation, deterioration, and ultimately the end of that institution as a viable part of the society it serves. With active, informed efforts to anticipate and adapt to changing needs, the institutional researcher can assist efforts to meet developing educational needs and to avoid, or at least minimize, the detrimental effects of retrenchment. A basic beginning can be achieved by the institutional researcher in a straightforward way; it is not too soon to begin that effort.

References

Bennett, B. J. "Computerized Budget Allocation Model." Unpublished computer programs, College of Engineering, Montana State University, Bozeman, Montana, 1972.

Caruthers, J. K., and Orwig, M. "Budgeting in Higher Education." *AAHE-ERIC/ Higher Education Research Report No. 3*. Washington, D.C.: American Association for Higher Education, 1979.

Dressel, P., and Associates. *Institutional Research in the University: A Handbook*. San Francisco: Jossey-Bass, 1971.

Halstead, D. K. *Higher Education Prices and Price Indexes*. (1978 supplement.) Washington, D.C.: U.S. Government Printing Office, 1978.

Schultze, C. L. *The Politics and Economics of Public Spending*. Washington, D.C.: Brookings Institution, 1968.

Southern Methodist University Institute of Technology. *1973 Annual Report*. Dallas, Tex.: Southern Methodist University Institute of Technology, 1973.

Wildavsky, A. *The Politics of the Budgeting Process*. (2nd ed.) Boston: Little, Brown, 1974.

Wm. A. Johnstone, professor emeritus at Montana State University, has taught at all levels in his forty-three years in education, from elementary science to the three course sequence in administration of higher education he now teaches in the doctoral program at M.S.U. His experience as an administrator has ranged from elementary principal to acting president of M.S.U. His major roles have been sixteen years as a school superintendent in Montana and thirteen years as administrative vice-president of M.S.U.; the latter role included institutional research and planning.

Institutions facing faculty reduction may look for "escape routes," such as early retirement or faculty re-deployment. Although all institutions should investigate these programs, only a few campuses are likely to lessen reduction pressures through these methods.

Escape Routes: Do They Exist?

Fred F. Harcleroad

The well-known, serious problems facing postsecondary education in the 1980s provide very limited opportunity in most institutions for escape from faculty reductions. Significant reductions-in-force have already affected many institutions throughout the United States. However, by forethought and adroit handling of critical factors, some institutions and individuals may avoid or mitigate particularly severe or difficult situations. A number of different, seemingly unrelated background topics must be considered in deciding among alternatives at a particular institution.

First, the great diversity of postsecondary institutions in the United States makes it impossible to generalize on a national or even a regional basis. These thousands of institutions differ greatly in their missions, funding sources, support levels, academic programs, mix of students, and patterns of governance. Clark and Youn (1976, pp. 41-43) have graphically portrayed the "persistence of institutional inequality" which results in a country in which there are "... rich institutions and poor ones, 'noble' ones and 'less-noble' places. In short, there will be extensive stratification of institutions.... Financial support comes from many sources, rather than the national treasury alone; autonomous private institutions adapt to different, specific clienteles; state colleges and universities reflect state and regional differences. Institutions are relatively exposed to market forces—for example, changing consumer interests and competition from other colleges and universities. Dispersed control has included a differentiation of sectors, and what one sector will not do, another will."

As a consequence, in the 1980s faculty reduction activities, likewise, will be varied. While a multi-campus state system may establish a common set of procedures and regulations, each of the church-related colleges, bible schools, and theological schools, for example, will react individually. In addition, the varied effects in the different regions and states will undoubtedly lead to wide variances among institutions in different geographic areas. These inequalities mean, of course, that some institutions will be affected much less than others and faculty reductions will vary greatly as a result.

Second, population in the United States is characterized by a wavelike structure, with crests and troughs, rather than by a steady flow or growth. Today, a sizable wave of people in the age sixty range is followed by a trough in the middle forties, and a huge towering wave in the early thirties is followed by a deep trough from age one to the middle twenties. In particular, changes in laws and mores relating to abortion have currently resulted in well over a million abortions a year. In turn, this leads to a more constant population, much smaller future waves, and significantly smaller potential for college attendance by the 18-22 age group. By the year 2000, nearly 40 percent of the population will be over 50 (over 70 million people), with approximately one third over 70. New concepts of life and career stages develop rapidly under such conditions, with considerable effect on demand for new or adaptive educational programs. In 1975, for example, 4 percent of those over 80 were employed full or part-time, and in 1980 it could easily be higher (Jones, 1978, p. 125). As individuals with two, three, or even four separate careers become more common, and new "schooling" becomes more necessary during such lifestyle changes, faculty members of colleges and universities may well have to adapt as much or more than other large groups.

Third, the minimal inflation of the 1950s has been replaced by the relatively high inflation and federal deficits of the Johnson, Nixon, and Carter years. Formerly adequate pension funds cannot provide adequately for inflated costs and longer lives. For example, a person retired in 1970 with a pension of $9,000 a year plus maximum Social Security benefits lost 25 percent of the purchasing power by 1977 and an almost similar additional loss by 1980.

Fourth, another major social problem is vitally affected by decisions in this area. Equal employment opportunity requires special attention to the needs of women, ethnic minorities, and older people. In this area postsecondary institutions have a particularly important role. Teaching and other forms of educational service have provided major opportunities for social mobility throughout the history of our nation. Thus any unique efforts to provide "escape routes" during this period of diminishing enrollments and of faculty reductions must be developed only after grave consideration of this critical factor. With fewer jobs available overall, the conflicting rights of these three groups could present difficult problems to both our governance systems and our courts. For example, in the Gault case (Flygare, 1978, pp. 711-712), the Court of Appeals ruled regarding forced retirement at age 65 that "teaching is a profession in which mental skills are vastly more important than physical ability. We cannot assume that a teacher's mental facilities diminish at age 65. On the contrary, . . . much in the way of knowledge and experience, so helpful to the educational profession, is often gained through years of practice." Flygare (1978, p. 712), as a result of this and related cases, feels that "American education at all levels would be well advised to begin thinking ahead to the day when teachers and professors will not be forced to retire at any age."

Fifth, in 1978, the Congress of the United States moved vigorously in this direction by passing the 1978 Amendments to the Age Discrimination in Employment Act, which raised the minimum age for mandatory retirement from 65 to 70, with few exceptions. For tenured college professors the implementation date of the law was delayed until July 1, 1982. Senator Claude Pepper, close to 80 years of age and a major author and supporter of the act has predicted further elimination of forced retirement and age discrimination in employment.

These five background areas greatly affect any adjustments and changes that colleges and universities may wish to make to ease problems caused by faculty reductions. This will be even more true in regard to any actions that may be considered alternatives or escape routes. The remainder of this chapter discusses these topics in three sections relating to (1) faculty career stages and development, (2) retirement laws, systems, and effects, and (3) implications for institutional research.

Faculty Career Stages and Development

The situation of college and university faculty in 1980 reflects the current social scene, but with some areas of concern that are even more severe. Inflation, of course, hits very hard at the salaries of all college and university personnel. Faculty and staff alike are affected by this "silent thief." Although overall compensation per work-hour almost doubled from 1968 to 1977, the increase in purchasing power amounted to 1 percent a year before taxes. However, higher pay levels lead to taxes at progressively higher rates and actually lower purchasing power. A family making $30,000 in 1970 needed $49,650 in 1978 to stay equal in pay but moved into a tax bracket 13 percent higher and with 7 percent less purchasing power. Lower salaries with less leeway are hit even harder in actual level of living. With support for higher education as a whole dropping due to increasing societal priorities for expenditures for energy, environment, and equality of all human services, the overall percent of state public funds going into colleges and universities has gone down regularly for several years. This has occurred in most states, even though enrollments have continued to increase during the same period. With expected large drops in enrollment after 1981-82 and potential enrollment decreases ranging up to 25 percent by 1990, additional funds needed to avoid faculty reductions will be hard to achieve (Parker, 1977, pp. 5, 7).

The resulting problems of faculty reduction can affect people differently, depending on the stage of their development. Baldwin (1979) has summarized a variety of studies and models of adult devvelopment periods, applicable to college faculty and based on five stages adapted from Levinson. These five stages are (1) entering the adult world, ages 22-28, assistant professor in the first three full years of college teaching; (2) the age-thirty transition, 28-33, an experienced assistant professor; (3) settling down, 33-40, and becoming one's own person during the late settling down period, 36-40, an associate professor; (4) mid-life transition, 40-45, and entering middle adulthood, 46-50, early period as a full professor; and (5) later adult transition, 60-65, a full professor within a few years of retirement. Of course, it is important also to add that many professional faculty live a full quarter or more of their lives in retirement (Mulanaphy, 1978, p. 1). This long life stage in retirement also has several developmental periods, but they have an extremely limited relationship to the problems of faculty reduction considered here.

The previous five stages, however, do have significant bearing. During the first early period one of the most possible "escape routes" will be to give up college and university teaching and research as a goal. This may be particularly true in professional areas such as medicine, law, design, pharmacy, or engineering, where other job opportunities are often better and material rewards may be greater and available faster. Even in liberal arts fields such as history or art this may be true as positions for archivists or museum directors develop. Also, in stages two and three, assistant professors and some associate professors with limited tenure or promotion opportunities may choose to move out of universities. It could be catastrophic for postsecondary institutions if many of the top prospective intellectual producers of the next 20-40 years make this choice. Conceivably, the most active creative ones might leave. Since a majority of faculty never produce another published volume after their dissertation (Ladd, 1979, p. 3), it could materially change the university if a significant part of the remainder would leave for other types of work. To avoid such a disaster, reward systems should be adapted in most of our 3,200 institutions (in all but 75-125 research universities) so that teachers can be rewarded (promoted in rank and given tenure plus merit raises) on the basis of evidence of continuing scholarly preparation in their teaching and of keeping up with developments in their fields.

A few specific examples of ideas for faculty development and funding of alternative routes still available to universities may be helpful. In the first stage, a faculty mentor/sponsorship has been reported by Blackburn (1979, p. 25) to be critical to the "launching of a productive career." This could be done on a more organized basis by concerned departments. The National Science Foundation (NSF) has proposed a number of programs designed to open up more avenues for science faculty to remain in postsecondary education, including: "(1) a national postdoctoral fellowship program with three-year awards to candidates who at the time of their application have not had their Ph.D. degree for more than one year. Fellows would choose their institutions and the investigator with whom they want to work. Support would come from NSF funds allotted to investigators for hiring postdoctoral fellows. (2) NSF Research Career Development Awards to universities for specified young scientists who have already demonstrated their research potential but are not established as independent investigators. These awards would extend up to five years, but the university would have to offer its holder a tenure-track position. (3) NSF Research Scientist Awards to faculty in their mid-career. These awards would be for three years and would support faculty in changing scientific fields or in intensifying research activity. The winners would have a leave of absence from normal university responsibilities. (4) National research professorships to individuals who have had distinguished scientific careers. These professorships would support the scientist for the rest of his research career and free him from university duties. The university would be expected to use its salary savings to employ young faculty in the same department" (Shulman, 1979, p. 23).

Some businesses have stepped up cooperative, re-education programs where faculty take leaves of absence to work in related fields while on leave from their institutional positions. This provides re-training for the faculty member and an entry position for a beginning faculty member. The National Endowment for the Humanities has taken the other tack, with business and foundation support, and provided postdoctoral (or almost completed) students with a summer program designed to prepare for business careers. Most of these persons then stayed in business careers (Shulman, p. 24). Some proposals have been made to increase staffing flexibility by hiring more part-time faculty, possibly in combination with part-time work in the region. This might help in some institutions, once again primarily in professional fields. In community colleges, however, hiring part-time faculty has been a way of life for many years. At the present time a majority of community college students and faculty are part-time, and additional moves in this direction could lead to serious problems (Lombardi, 1975, pp. 9-19). Studies show that full-time teachers at community colleges feel threatened by part-time faculty who teach for less, tolerate larger classes, and replace regular teachers during strikes (Obetz, 1976, p. 25). Greatly enlarged use of part-time faculty, if carried on by other institutions on a large scale, conceivably could cause similar reactions.

Clearly, a variety of faculties and institutions might profit marginally from various types of leaves, additional research fellowships, cooperative training efforts with business or government agencies, and packaging part-time loads with related but extra-institutional work. All these ideas must be tried, plus others that will be developed. However, at best they appear limited in meeting possible demands in many institutions for future faculty reductions.

Retirement Laws, Systems, and Effects

Retirement Laws. On April 6, 1978, an amendment to the Age Discrimination in Employment Act of 1967 was signed into law. It prohibited mandatory retirement below age 70 for most public and private employees after January 1, 1978. However, for tenured college professors, the effective date of the law is July 1, 1982. For employees in groups covered by collective bargaining pension plans and based on retirement at 65 (which could include those in some higher education institutions), the effective date was delayed until the end of the agreement or January 1, 1980, whichever came first. For policy-making executives with employer-financed retirement benefits exceeding $27,000 yearly, exclusive of social security, retirement at age 65 may be continued. For federal employees, the current mandatory retirement age of 70 was removed, and they can work as long as they wish while performing adequately on the job.

In addition, a number of states have adopted similar laws. For example, California abolished mandatory retirement at any age, as of January 1, 1980, for private or public employees, except those in public law enforcement or firefighting. Similar laws for state and local employees exist in Montana, Maine, and Florida (Cook, 1979, p. 12). Corwin and Gross (1979, p. 5) found that eleven states (California, Connecticut, Delaware, Hawaii, Maine, Massachusetts, Minnesota, New Hampshire, Ohio, Rhode Island, and South Carolina) had existing state laws in 1979 that prevented institutions from delaying the effective date for tenured faculty to the July 1, 1982 set in the federal amendments.

Clearly, the direction in retirement policies is to continue and extend the teaching periods of current faculty rather than to reduce them. During a time of potential need for faculty reduction, this exacerbates the problem. Older, senior faculty normally have the highest salaries, and percentage raises can lead to fewer positions available on the faculty as a whole. Likewise, such policies could lead to attacks on the tenure system, since tenure without mandatory retirement could seriously restrict entry into the profession.

The Department of Labor is charged with the administration of the 1978 amendments. In issuing the implementing regulations it provided as follows (King and Cook, 1980, pp. 103-5, 245-247):

1. Institutions can retain a "normal" retirement age below 70. Defined benefit plans do not have to give additional credit for years of service or salary increases after the "normal" age. They may discontinue employer contributions also.

2. Faculty members hired within five years of the "normal" age do not have to be included in the retirement plan.

3. Fringe benefits such as group life insurance may be reduced, and health insurance costs may be reduced after age sixty-five when maintained by Medicare. Disability insurance reductions prior to age 70 are limited to benefits based on age-related costs.

4. The regulations do allow a number of flexible arrangements that could assist in employment policies during periods of possible reductions, such as financially-attractive early retirement programs or phased-retirement arrangements combining reductions in work load and pay with a start-up of a portion of retirement income.

Other similar arrangements could make a considerable difference in openness of the system during the next decade. Currently, the median age of full-time faculty is only 42, with 15.6 percent over age 55 and only 6.8 percent over age 60. These data coincide with Department of Labor data on the entire work force in the United States. The largest group of full-time faculty is still in their thirties and early forties. Many are without tenure, since the median age for full-time tenured faculty is 48, with about one quarter over 55. This figure is skewed by about one fourth of the institutions (mostly private, small, undergraduate institutions) with more than 30 percent of their full-time faculty over 55 (Corwin, 1978, p. 1). This latter group will be vitally affected, and very soon, by the amended retirement law.

Collective bargaining by and for public employees has increased dramatically during the past decade. This increase kept overall union membership growing slightly even though it dropped steadily in business and industry. Significant numbers of organized faculties in colleges and universities, particularly community colleges, now bargain regularly. Increasingly, faculty and staff unions may stress seniority to protect the positions of their members. Many protagonists for unions also support the cause of minorities and women in their attempts to break down white male predominance on campuses. These two conflicting goals will lead to some traumatic situations—but seniority and continuity until retirement for current tenured union members may well prevail over other considerations. This problem could be particularly difficult for the American Association of University Professors, since their 1940 *Statement of Principles on Academic Freedom and Tenure* emphasizes that once tenure is earned, it continues until age of retirement.

With regard to longevity of our population, faculty members tend to live even longer than many other groups. Some very valuable data on this point comes from the Teachers Insurance and Annuity Association. Their current annuity tables are drawn from actual experience with their own annuitants. These tables show an average life expectancy at age 65 of 17 years for a male and 21 years for a female. These figures are 3 to 5 years greater for each group than for the population as a whole and indicate that higher education retirement plans will pose even greater problems in adjustment than those in business and industry.

Retirement Systems. At the time the federal Amendments were passed, current policies regarding mandatory retirement in higher education institutions indicated wide differences among institutions. Although almost two thirds of the institutions had mandated retirement at age 65 or earlier, and 36 percent had set retirement at some age over 65 (with 15 percent at 70), while 9 percent (with only 3 percent of the total of the faculty of the institutions) had no mandatory age. Also, many institutions with retirement ages set below 70 allowed extensions on a year-to-year basis up to 70 and even beyond for 30 percent of those allowing such extensions (Corwin, 1978, p. 2).

In such a situation, professors' attitudes toward retirement can be critical. In 1978, Palmer and Patton reported pertinent data for institutions classified as (1) research universities, (2) doctoral universities, (3) other universities and colleges, and (4) two-year colleges. In this study, less than one quarter of the institutions provided retirement at 70 or older. However, 31 percent of public research universities currently had mandatory retirement ages at 70 or over. Moreover, 88 percent of the public research universities allowed extensions up to or past 70 years of age. Age distributions of faculty were found to be similar to other studies reviewed earlier. Differences in mandatory retirement were not closely related to age group distribution. In public and private research universities, only 1-2 percent of faculty were over 66 years of age, and only slightly more than 6 percent were between 61 and 65. In regard to faculty plans for age of retirement, 24 percent of those in research universities planned to retire after age 67, 55 percent between ages 64 and 66, and 21 percent by age 63. In those research universities with mandatory retirement at age 70 or later, there were 44 percent who planned early retirement between ages 64 and 66. The lowest planned retirement ages were in two year colleges, with 57 percent by age 63 and all of the remainder by age 64 to 66. None of the two-year colleges allowed retirement at age 70 or later. A variety of incentive early-retirement plans were suggested, for consideration by faculty ages 50 to 62. Plans suggested included early retirement of three, four to six, or seven years in advance with (1) an assured one-half of annual salary, (2) assured full pension benefits as of mandatory retirement age, (3) assured full annual salary, and (4) assured part-time employment. In almost all cases, faculty members in research institutions were less inclined to retire early. In fact, only 28 percent of such faculty were positive about accepting full salary for retirement seven years in advance in a mandatory retirement plan at age 70, and 37 percent preferred to work to age 70 rather than retire with full pay at any earlier age. Approximately 60 percent in all categories, however, *would* accept some type of inducement to retire early. Probably the least expensive would be "assured part-time employment," the only incentive of the four suggested that provides no extra money payment for less or no work.

Effects of Early Retirement Systems. A number of key problem areas are very apparent primarily in the two major categories of (1) personnel administration and (2) institutional budgeting and finance. However, they materially affect all other aspects of institutional operation, including offices of institutional research.

Palmer and Patton (1978, pp. 19-20) studied a number of early retirement plans, breaking them down into five categories, as follows: "(1) actuarial reduction (for example, increasing the entitlement at age 62 to 90 percent of the normal entitlement rather than a much heavier percentage deduction); (2) a pension supplement (providing additional funding from the institutional general funds to supplement the normal retirement income available at any given age); (3) part-time employment allowed after retirement, with no deductions from the full retirement benefits; (4) continuation of perquisites (for example, continued office use or a continuation of selected employee benefits); (5) combinations of the above options."

Supplementing the pension (category 2) appears to be the most successful in bringing about early retirement, but none of the plans have been strikingly successful. To date, early retirement has had only "modest impact upon the age composition of the faculty" (Palmer and Patton, 1978, p. 20).

In his study of early incentives, Patton found that four research universities (the University of California, Stanford University, Indiana University, and the Massachusetts Institute of Technology) had sufficient experience with such plans to merit extensive case study of the institutions and of approximately one half (fifty-two) of the early retirees. Most retired about four years early because of interests outside their university responsibilities. Forty percent were fatigued by academic pressures or no longer enjoyed their work. Only 27 percent indicated it was the early retirement option that made it financially possible to retire. Finally, 20 percent had a disability or health problem that contributed to the decision to retire early.

Almost all of the early retirees were satisfied with their decision, and 90 percent would do the same again. Significantly, 88 percent had no material change in their standard of living. Many found their "spendable" income higher after retirement, partly because they paid no income taxes on social security or previously taxed personal contributions to pension plans, and because large personal obligations and university-connected costs are behind them. Also, retirement was still recent enough so that inflation had not yet made a significant dent in life styles. In addition, 83 percent continued professional activity of some type, and 71 percent had been "gainfully employed." Undoubtedly, this pension supplement greatly helped to ease the changeover and maintain their life styles.

From an administrative point of view, the methods of implementation resulted in negative reactions that developed because of three factors:

- The loss of the early retiree's position from the department involved because it reverted back to the university administration.
- A disappointment with the amount of funds released in the cases where the department retained the position.
- A general dissatisfaction with the way in which the program was administered.

As a result of this dissatisfaction, departments feel little incentive to encourage early retirement. If the result is loss of a position or insufficient funds to employ a completely satisfactory replacement, there is no logical reason to support early retirement activity. Even when part-time employment is elected, administrative unhappiness often results. Early retirees usually think their part-time teaching will be a small seminar, and the department head often has large introductory courses in mind. Also, office space often ends up as an issue, since the senior, now part-time professor still wants a full-time private office.

From the overall institutional viewpoint, it is critical to provide a well-coordinated, clear, and understandable early retirement plan with no ambiguities. Legal counsel on the system and appropriate methods of approach are necessary to avoid some hard feelings and possible litigation. Perceptive department administrators should know which faculty might be interested, if the department heads are well-briefed on the options and on the entire system. In addition, a voluntary but complete retirement preparation program should be organized and operated. The best ones combine one-to-one counseling with group sessions on (1) the institution's retirement benefits, both pension and non-pension, (2) health benefits and care, (3) legal affairs, (4) financial and income planning, (5) housing, and (6) use of free time in retirement, including volunteer services and organizations for retired people (Mulanaphy, 1978, pp. vii-76). If phased retirement is possible, it should be fully explained. Also, any possibilities for work outside the university should be pointed out. For example, retirement often is not required for such persons as writers, artists, doctors, realtors, or farmers.

Serious personnel problems can develop, however, if early retirement plans and other aspects of extending pension plans to age 70 or beyond are not handled well. Undoubtedly, there will be increased performance evaluation of tenured faculty and staff. If competency is the criterion rather than age, there must be an increase in this touchy, difficult task. Better and more consistent performance records will be necessary if any action is to be taken. This will be even more critical if there is no mandatory retirement age and employees continue so long as they demonstrate ability to perform the functions of the job adequately and the employer is satisfied with the quality of the work performed.

Until 1982, institutions can test their instruments and procedures for humaneness, efficiency, and legality. This will be quite important for overall employee morale. Those who retire early must estimate many intangibles, including their health, possible longevity, potential and unpredictable effects of inflation, possible part-time work, and the effects of changing from a demanding, daily work effort to a less demanding, totally voluntary effort. For compulsive, discipline-oriented faculty members these decisions can be especially traumatic. A pre-retirement preparation program is essential.

Difficult financial and budgeting problems also will result from these changes. Higher costs will result from the need for better record systems for performance evaluation of competency. Salary costs will be higher for older faculty at the top of the ranges. Cost of living increases for this group will raise total amounts significantly—with great impact in the 2000s as the wave of younger faculty reach their late sixties and early seventies. Fringe benefit costs will escalate rapidly and immediately. A recent Teachers Insurance and Annuity Association estimate of disability insurance and income protection, based on a sample of ten institutions, indicated that premiums might increase as much as 50 percent unless they are terminated at the current normal retirement age at each of the institutions. Life insurance costs per $1,000 of coverage are twenty times greater for a male of age 70 than for one of 30, and five times greater than at age 50 (Heim, 1978, pp. 10-11). Any program of induced early retirement will also have extra costs, even though there is an attempt to pay increased pensions from savings on the salary of a replacement.

Clearly, the effects of the changing retirement laws will pose some difficult options for all institutions (Jenny, 1979, pp. 1-6). The greatest problems will probably be providing openings for younger, varied faculty members with their new ideas and maintaining curricular and research vitality. Some form of induced early retirement with a financial incentive will be necessary to provide for such flexibility. If the choice remains primarily a faculty rather than administrative option, faculty will not oppose it; a few may retire early. If this should happen, the tight faculty employment market of the next ten years might be alleviated a little because of the new retirement laws.

Implications for Institutional Research

Decisions regarding the organization of faculty development programs, special plans for encouraging early retirement, and other related topics will require extensive background information. In addition to basic information, policy options regarding critical issues will be of great importance. Offices of institutional research within all types of postsecondary institutions need to gear up (if not already in operation) to provide both the basic data and the policy options.

Complete systems providing information on all the key data elements in the administration of an institution will be important. However, basic data regarding faculty and staff personnel will be the most critical elements needed in meeting these particular problems.

The possible list of useful studies is limitless. Those that follow illustrate some of the key areas in which studies may well be needed:

1. Age patterns of faculty in institutions or in institutional systems need to be studied in relation to developmental stages and academic ranks. Such data can be critical to the development of sabbaticals, with emphasis on the age groups that will profit most from this activity and provide openings for new faculty to be appointed, at least on a temporary basis.

2. Changing age patterns of students on the campus or in external locations should be studied. Will "older" faculty profess to the young (18-22), or will the age range of students increase (35-80+) as the faculty ages?

3. There should be preliminary studies of potential faculty retirements by department, and by specialty within the discipline. Are there specific subject areas in which early retirement might be especially encouraged through financial incentives, the development of part-time split positions, and other comparable routes? Are there specific disciplines in which good, young faculty from groups such as ethnic minorities or women should be of particular value—and where there are strong possibilities for retention in the future? From a social point of view, it could be particularly unfortunate to employ them only to have to cast them out due to forthcoming requirements for faculty reduction.

4. Studies of older members of the faculty should be made to see if they are interested in taking courses at the institution, which might prepare them for optimum retirement activity (either paid or volunteer). This could be combined with a possible study of plans of faculty members regarding their time of retirement. An option to encourage such activity might be an offer of free tuition, along with a slightly lighter load. A knowledge of actual costs of various programs with low enrollments and rising costs will be extremely useful as institutional and general expenditures per student increase. It will be important to pin-point those areas moving most rapidly in this direction.

5. Institutions should define "financial exigency?" Courts have made it clear that termination of faculty because of "financial exigency" is proper. However, definitions of this concept and its application at various institutions for various departments and programs will be essential.

6. Fringe benefit programs and their costs need to be documented for individual institutions. As the average age of faculty

grows, estimates of specific costs for particular fringe benefits must be known. This will be particularly true in determining whether such benefits as disability pensions are continued after normal retirement age.

7. Merit evaluation systems will become increasingly critical and measures of "productivity" of some type will be required. The new, more flexible retirement policies without any mandatory retirement ages will place increasing emphasis on plans of this type. Continuing record systems will be a basic part of the information system in the future.

8. Analysis of the faculty by fields will be very useful, including data comparing faculty with and without other potential work outlets.

9. Studies are needed of campus atmosphere and morale, in order to see if it contributes to creative teaching and productive research.

10. Joint efforts with the personnel department will be most desirable. For example, appropriate data can provide the basis for planning the pre-retirement counseling program that the department should carry out.

Some Final Points

The thirty-fifth decade in which postsecondary education has existed in the United States could and should be one of the three or four best decades for this important social institution. The enrollment reductions and decreasing support for higher education expenditures that developed in the 1970s can present problems. In 1978, the elimination of mandatory retirement darkened the outlook and increased the possibility of faculty reductions. Some institutions will be affected far more than others. Efforts to adapt to changing populations could be quite important. This will be the first decade of thirty-five in which the "masses" will be elderly. Fortunately, as the population has aged, the existing productivity of our society has for the first time in history provided leisure time and publically supported retirement for these masses of people. Of course, existing productivity levels will undoubtedly be needed in the United States if such public-supported retirement systems are to continue.

Finally, the actions of the faculty themselves will be a very important and basic factor in affecting the needs for faculty reduction on a given campus. Clearly, some institutions attract students—

and in the next decades could maintain their current enrollments even though the overall pool of students drops appreciably. A key element in this particular set of institutions could well be a dedicated faculty that operates in a highly positive way, personalizing its educational program for its students.

References and Sources

In the area of retirement plans and benefits the highly professional staff of the Teachers Insurance and Annuity Association have for decades published many of the basic documents. In the present critical period this continues to be true and the author of this chapter profited greatly from their providing copies of all their related publications. Several of the most valuable ones are included below.

Baldwin, R. "Adult and Career Development: What Are Implications For Faculty?" In *Faculty Career Development*. Washington, D.C.: American Association for Higher Education, 1979.

Blackburn, R. T. "Academic Careers: Patterns and Possibilities." In *Faculty Career Development*. Washington, D.C.: American Association for Higher Education, 1979.

Bowen, H. R. *Academic Compensation*. New York: Teachers Insurance and Annuity Association, 1978.

Clark, B. R., and Youn, T. I. K. *Academic Power in the United States*. Research Report No. 3. Washington, D.C.: American Association for Higher Education, 1976.

Cook, T. J. *Public Retirement Systems*. New York: Teachers Insurance and Annuity Association, 1979.

Corwin, T. M. "A Research Perspective on Mandatory Retirement." In *Changing Retirement Policies*. Washington, D.C.: American Association for Higher Education, 1978.

Corwin, T. M., and Gross, A. C. "Higher Education Responds to Changing Retirement Laws: A Followup Report." In *Policy Briefs*. Washington, D.C.: American Council on Education, 1979.

Flygare, T. J. "Mandatory Retirement is Fading Fast: Will Tenure be Next?" *Phi Delta Kappan*. June, 1978, pp. 711-712.

Heim, P. "Implications of Mandatory Retirement Legislation for Institutions of Higher Education." In *Changing Retirement Policies*. Washington, D.C.: American Association for Higher Education, 1978.

Jenny, H., Heim, P., and Hughes, G. C. *Another Challenge: Age 70 Retirement in Higher Education*. New York: Teachers Insurance and Annuity Association, 1979.

Jones, T. (Ed.). "Going Strong in Your 80s." *Quest*, March-April 1978, pp. 113-128.

King, F. P., and Cook, T. J. *Benefit Plans in Higher Education*. New York: Columbia University Press, 1980.

Ladd, E. C., Jr. "The Work Experience of American College Professors: Some Data and Argument." In *Faculty Career Development*. Washington, D.C.: American Association for Higher Education, 1979.

Lombardi, J. *Part-Time Faculty in Community Colleges.* Topical Paper No. 54. Los Angeles: ERIC Clearinghouse for Junior Colleges, 1975.

Mulanaphy, J. M. *Retirement Preparation in Higher Education.* New York: Teachers Insurance and Annuity Association, 1978.

Obetz, R. M. "The Part-Time Humanities Instructor." *Faculty Characterstics.* Los Angeles: ERIC Clearinghouse for Junior Colleges, 1976.

Palmer, D. D., and Patton, C. V. "Faculty Attitudes Toward Early Retirement." In *Changing Retirement Policies.* Washington, D.C.: American Association for Higher Education, 1978.

Parker, G. *Higher Education Enrollments: Implications for the 1980's.* Topical Paper No. 8. Office of Research and Study in Higher Education, University of Arizona, June 1977.

Shulman, C. H. *Old Expectations, New Realities: The Academic Profession Revisited.* Research Report No. 2. Washington, D.C.: American Association for Higher Education, 1979.

Weathersby, R. P., and Tarule, J. M. *Adult Development: Implications for Higher Education.* Research Report No. 4. Washington, D.C.: American Association for Higher Education, 1980.

Fred F. Harcleroad is a professor of higher education at the Center for the Study of Higher Education, University of Arizona, and director of the Center. Previously, he served as president of the American College Testing Program, as founding president of California State University at Hayward, and as academic dean of San Jose State University. He has served as consultant on organization, finance, accreditation, and evaluation for a dozen states and many higher education institutions. Harcleroad is author or editor of many books and monographs, including Assessment of Colleges and Universities.

The problems related to faculty retrenchment and planning for enrollment declines within the University of Wisconsin system have been considerable; some valuable lessons have been learned as a result.

Faculty Retrenchment: The Experience of the University of Wisconsin System

Cyrena Pondrom

Although the University of Wisconsin (UW)–Madison has escaped retrenchment of tenured faculty, more than half of the system institutions have not, and planning for the possibility of faculty reductions has been a constant requirement for each of the fifteen system institutions for most of the last decade. For a variety of historical reasons, the experience of the UW System may be especially useful to faculty and administrations contemplating the prospect of faculty reductions. Institutions in the system are quite diverse, including a university made up of two-year campuses (the Center System), a number of non-doctoral institutions that originated as teachers' colleges, an extension institution, a large urban doctoral campus (Milwaukee), and a top-ranked national research institution (Madison). Among the non-doctoral universities, the missions of several have also been diverse; for example, one has achieved a national recognition in training instructors in vocational and industrial arts (UW-Stout), and another has implemented an experimental curriculum focused on environmental concerns (UW-Green Bay). Some have admitted students with minimum requirements and others have, attracted chiefly students with good academic records in an array of college preparatory courses. Some institutions originated in the middle of the last century, and others in the middle of this one. In the early 1970s, all were brought together, with their disparate histories, to function within a common system policy framework.

Different institutions in the newly merged system had widely varying experiences in accommodating fiscal austerity. Since the efforts at reduction of instructional costs were carried out under the overall policy supervision of a single system administration, the differences in retrenchment experience may more clearly reflect the implications of different past personnel practices (and different institutional types) than would otherwise be the case.

Summary of the UW System Faculty Retrenchment Experience

In 1972-73, the abrupt state reduction of funding for the four-year institutions with declining enrollments precipitated one of the earlier recent layoff actions for tenured faculty among major institutions. In May 1973, eighty-eight tenured faculty were notified of layoff effective one year later. In addition, 344 instructional staff with two years service or less were terminated in May 1973, following proper notice periods of varying lengths, and about 155 probationary staff with more than two years service were given notice of nonretention effective in May 1974. Although untenured staff were terminated with proper notice, and thus not laid off, many of them (although certainly not all) would have been continued had there been no fiscal emergency.

Of the original eighty-eight tenured faculty affected, fifty-six had their layoff designations rescinded as attrition and other economy measures made possible their retention; nine resigned to take other positions; six were relocated to other system institutions as tenured faculty; and one retired. Sixteen remained on layoff status in October 1980, including four who hold non-tenure track (visiting or academic staff) positions in the system. Most of the other twelve are employed outside the UW System and have elected to retain their layoff status.

In May 1974, thirty-four more tenured faculty were given notice of layoff effective in May 1975. Twenty-nine of those layoffs were eventually rescinded, three resigned in exchange for a year's leave at full pay, and two were actually laid off. One remained on layoff status in October 1980, and one was deceased. Thus the total number of tenured faculty on layoff status from the University of Wisconsin System at the end of 1980 was seventeen, all as a result of actions taken in 1973 and 1974. Nine of the fourteen institutions judged it necessary to deal with fiscal austerity by layoff actions. Of the original eighty-eight, twenty-three were at Oshkosh, seventeen at Whitewater, fifteen at Platteville, twelve at Stevens Point, eight at Eau Claire, six at LaCrosse, four at Stout, two in the Center System, and one at River Falls. Several of these institutions managed to work out the economic emergency before actual layoffs occurred or soon thereafter. The sixteen who remained on layoff were at three institutions: Oshkosh (eleven), Platteville (four), and Stevens Point (one). Only three institutions instituted layoff actions in 1974—Stevens Point (sixteen), Platteville (ten), and Whitewater (eight); and all five who did not have their layoffs rescinded were at Stevens Point (Karges, 1980).*

The University of Wisconsin–Madison, Extension, Superior, Green Bay, Parkside, and Milwaukee did not experience faculty layoffs. However, each of these institutions absorbed reductions in ways that affected staffing patterns. For example, at the outset of the retrenchment period, the UW–Madison absorbed a sharp budget reduction by abolishing a campus level student services unit, with attendant terminations and reassignments. In addition, extramurally funded academic staff at Madison were (and continue to be) laid off for proven fiscal exigency when other alternatives did not exist.

Subsequently, the system has undertaken a series of extensive and careful projections of future work load requirements. Enrollment projections for the system as a whole in mid-1978 showed a "worst case" enrollment loss of up to 31 percent for undergraduates during the period 1980-1993, or 21 percent for all programs ("UW-System Total: Actual and Estimated Enrollments; Traditional Age Pool-Constant," 1978). As a result of these expectations, the system

---

*The author is very much indebted to Steven Karges for providing detailed information about the numbers and distribution of faculty affected by layoff, as well as for his reflections about the implications of actions taken at that time.

and individual institutions have been engaged in very detailed analyses of enrollment trends at an institutional level and in planning for matching faculty staffing levels to enrollment and support levels in the 1980s. As part of this effort, the UW–Madison developed in 1977 a "faculty flow model" that projected the impact of enrollment levels from 1977 to 1996 on decisions about promotion, nonretention, tenure density, and external hiring of both junior and senior staff.

In addition, during this period policy and administrative rules covering appointment, use, retention, and layoff of academic staff (including non-ladder or non-track instructional staff) were adopted, formal retrenchment provisions for faculty (persons who are tenured or on tenure-track) were brought into being, and general faculty personnel rules were updated and codified.

Observations from the UW System Experience

Several general observations are possible on the basis of this history and the experience of the utility (or occasional inutility) of actions taken in response to these events.

First, severely reduced economic circumstances do not affect all types of institutions in the same way. Moreover, the personnel practices that have been traditional in an institution may be even more important than the type of institution in being correlated with the need for layoffs. A review of some reasons for why this appears to be so, with the assumed clarity of hindsight, is presented in the following section.

Second, faculty-flow studies developed as a result of these experiences strongly indicate that fiscal austerity is unlikely to affect similarly the different types of institutions within the system in the future, even though their personnel practices are becoming much more similar. It is important to carry out such studies and give them broad internal publicity, both to relieve in some institutions a "seige mentality" and to assist the faculty of all institutions in understanding the measures necessary to match resources with needs.

Third, when faculty reductions are inevitable but still some time off, there are basically only two general strategies that are available to achieve a smaller faculty: reducing long-term commitments long in advance and laying off tenured faculty when the time comes. Because each has profound implications for the fabric of institutional life, an examination of the ramifications of each strategy is presented later in this discussion.

Fourth, when strategies for avoidance have come to an end and layoffs must occur, there are some practical actions that will help contain the damage.

Fifth, some forms of elaboration of the campus governance structure can help to enable institutions to cope with retrenchment. The development of detailed written policies governing retrenchment practices (as well as many other personnel rules) did make staffing decisions more orderly and enabled them to be better related to future needs. It also, perhaps indirectly, made personnel decisions more cumbersome and time consuming. But there has been no repetition of the need to lay off tenured faculty, and there is considerable subjective evidence that there is greater attention paid by everyone at the time of a tenure commitment to its long-term implications.

The Impact of Personnel Practices

Both actual experience in the UW System and detailed projections of institutional staffing patterns for the next two decades make it extremely clear that anticipated retrenchment will not be borne uniformly by all institutions.

First, the UW System experience suggests that institutions with a pattern of giving tenure to most staff members will suffer much more quickly than those with a pattern of admitting only a (potentially variable) proportion of probationary staff to tenure. At the time of retrenchment action in 1972-73, the Wisconsin State University (WSU) System* and the University of Wisconsin** had just been directed by the state to merge and still operated under two different sets of personnel rules. In the WSU schools, tenure was, by state law, automatic upon completion of a fourth year of teaching. In UW schools the probationary period was seven years, and a significant proportion of junior faculty were, in fact, not retained. A 2.5 percent per year budget reduction (a "productivity cut") affected all institutions in the 1972-1974 biennium, and most institutions experienced some enrollment drops from 1969 to 1972-73. Nonetheless, none of the former UW universities were initially affected by layoff actions.

Second, the potential for reaching termination of tenured and

*Eau Claire, LaCrosse, Oshkosh, Platteville, River Falls, Stevens Point, Stout, Superior and Whitewater.
**Madison, Milwaukee, Green Bay, Parkside, Extension. In addition, in the merged System, 14 two-year campuses from both systems took a place as a single, independent institution, the UW Center System.

tenure track faculty was further reduced at both Madison and Milwaukee because of the presence of some part-time or temporary, off-ladder instructional staff on annual or shorter appointments. Although somewhat comparable positions existed in some other of the system's institutions, such appointments were relatively infrequent. In addition, both institutions, but especially Madison, appointed significant numbers of teaching assistants (TA's). Some enrollment loss could be absorbed by reduction of TA appointments. This alternative was only of moderate significance for three reasons. As with faculty, a reduction of TA appointments was possible only for new or temporary TA's because of the existence of three-year contracts for non-probationary TA's on regular appointments, a guarantee under the collective bargaining agreement then in existence between the UW–Madison and the Teaching Assistants Association. If increases in "productivity" in a university mean a rise in class sizes or class loads, then the 2.5 percent productivity cuts could not be shared by TA's and faculty alike, because the Teaching Assistants Association's contract set a limit on class size in TA-taught sections and established a fixed load. And more importantly, departments with few alternative resources for student support were reluctant to reduce TA appointments more than the minimum absolutely necessary because of the likelihood of forcing students out of graduate school.

Third, it was clear that the largest institutions had a much greater opportunity to absorb short-term cut backs through voluntary separation, which was 1.81 percent per year at Madison for senior staff and 5.52 percent per year for junior faculty, apart from normal non-retentions.

Conclusions from Faculty Flow Models

Comparison of future projections for the UW–Madison, derived from the twenty-year faculty flow model mentioned earlier, with those of other system institutions bears a somewhat similar message. If the UW–Madison maintains its current voluntarily established patterns of non-retention, voluntary separation, promotion, and outside hiring at the senior level, the tenure density (computed on a campus-wide basis) will peak at 80 percent in 1980 and decrease again in 1987. These projections assume a constant teacher-student ratio (16:1), retirement by existing staff at age seventy, no enrollment increases, and steady (but not extreme) enrollment drops between 1989 and 1996. By this date a bulge in retirements will cushion the enrollment decline. Projections for some other system institutions look substantially more pessimistic.

Projections such as these suggest that both the problems and the courses of action are different for different types of institutions. Informal consultations with administrators at several similar universities have tentatively suggested that the ages, rates of promotion, non-retention, voluntary separation, and enrollment projections at Madison are not really atypical for institutions of its kind. What faculty and deans within the institution have consistently found most striking about the model's results is the relatively high number of cumulative new hires that will be permitted campus-wide over a twenty year period, if current personnel practices are maintained: 2,280 by 1996.

If system-wide policies permit and hiring can be balanced campus-wide, then large, long-established institutions, with competitive promotion practices and no special circumstances causing immediate and precipitous enrollment declines, will probably not reach a state where layoff of faculty is necessary. Instead, voluntary turnover (a significant number in a very large faculty even where rates are quite low), normal non-retentions, and a peak in retirements between 1987 and 1996 will hold the impact of enrollment drops to tolerable levels.

Of course, there is a catch. Hiring is not done on a campus-wide but on a disciplinary or departmental basis. Student enrollment patterns are significantly different from what they were when faculty expansion was rapid. To make the projection as optimistic as it first appears when looked at from a campus-wide perspective, resources to meet growing work loads would have to be denied to expanding or new areas until attrition in "overstocked" areas made possible a shift in funds. Alternatively, replacement would be frozen and faculty would be non-retained for fiscal reasons (or even laid off) in departments of enrollment decline, while funds were still being pumped into expanding areas. Either of these alternatives, strictly followed, sets the stage for internecine warfare between have and have-not departments and has serious implications for maintenance of strength in some departments. There are advocates for both positions, however, and some faculty contracts—like that at Oakland University for example, as discussed in the chapter by Colleen Dolan-Greene, treat the layoff of faculty to maintain specified teacher-student ratios in each discipline as a "normal" and anticipated practice.

Much of the enrollment shift has been away from humanities departments, which in some institutions have often had a higher number of assigned contact hours and a higher student-teacher ratio. In these circumstances, an informed faculty is sure to generate some demand to let the enrollment shifts more evenly distribute teaching loads. Against this, an administrator is forced to balance the demands from departments receiving students to add resources to meet new work load requirements. In addition, by no means all areas of expanding student enrollment have previously been the beneficiary of lower contact-hour patterns.

On one conclusion, though, most administrators would agree. Whatever the conflicting priorities that must be resolved, the alternatives for action in this situation are less bitter than those giving institutions no recourse but to cut tenured faculty.

It is partly for this reason that development of careful projections concerning future staffing patterns are nearly as important for institutions that can avoid retrenchment actions as for those that cannot. Much has been written about coming losses of students, and faculty usually have no way to evaluate how much their own institutions will be affected. Faculty who think layoffs may be just around the corner, when they are not, suffer just as much morale loss as if their fears were true. And in the exercise of their governance responsibilities, these faculty may fail to recommend important appointments that could strengthen the institution.

Even in universities with very large projected numbers of hiring opportunities, faculty need an honest and open accounting of what sort of shifts in work load among departments must be faced. Administrations that do not acquaint faculty with such information available through a simple faculty flow model are passing up an opportunity to insure a much broader consensus and support for needed staffing actions (potentially to the detriment both of morale and of judicious decision-making where faculty participate in personnel decisions).

Choosing Courses of Action

Where overall reductions in faculty size are unavoidable, experience in the UW System offers some basis for choosing courses of action that avoid needlessly traumatic responses to fiscal exigency.

In the first place—self-evident as it may seem—universities should undertake layoff of tenured faculty only when such action is genuinely unavoidable. Some of the UW System layoff designations were issued to give a full year of notice to faculty who would be affected by a proposed "user fee." Subsequently, this method of funding widely expanded numbers of university programs was not adopted, and layoff notices for affected faculty were rescinded. One chancellor in an affected institution said that he would run the risk of letting all the plaster fall from the ceiling and every floor go uncleaned before he would again issue layoff designations he might eventually rescind. The speaker made an important point. Even where the cuts in non-personnel services would be too deep to be preferable to layoffs, it may be better to run that risk if there is a realistic possibility that the fiscal exigency may not be severe enough to require either action. The antagonisms and loss of morale generated by layoff actions are so severe that they continue to affect faculty-administration relationships and other aspects of institutional governance long after actual layoffs have been avoided or concluded. However, in some circumstances this strategy runs the risk of maximizing the possibility that cuts will be deep, since in a few states only the political pressure generated by actual layoffs has been a real deterrent to further legislative cuts (Johnson and Mortimer, 1977).

The same effect may be accomplished, without the potential of the grave consequences of unacceptably deep reductions in library, utility, or other essential non-personnel services, if the institution takes action well in advance of the need to plan for reduced staffing levels. It is neither original nor profound to stress that the objective of such planning is preserving the ability to reduce staffing levels without breaking contractual commitments, that is, in the magic word of these discussions, "flexibility." The key is no less significant because many have thought of it.

Such flexibility can be maintained in most cases by appointing some instructional staff in fixed-term positions, by making use of visiting staff, by conducting a review for promotion that allocates the few available tenured positions only to the most qualified, by implementing faculty development or retraining activities that prepare existing faculty for future needs, by reliance on adjunct staff, and, of course, by leaving vacated positions unfilled. A variety of other approaches can help in special circumstances, but the basic ones, clearly, are fixed-term appointments and a promotional system that restricts advancement to tenure.

If the measures are clear, why is the problem so difficult? The answer is, in its barest outline, that initiation of such procedures may profoundly alter the traditions, standards, code of behavior, and social fabric of an institution. When faculty have consistently been advanced to tenure when they have met certain requirements, introduction of a selection procedure that retains only the leaders on a widely variable scale changes the relationships and expectations of all staff. Probationary staff who are better qualified than some tenured staff may not be retained. Easy relationships between junior and senior staff breakdown, particularly where the faculty themselves largely determine whether an individual is kept on or let go. New and popular specialities in a department may be starved for staff, while older and now less exciting areas of specialization are overstocked.

Indeed, some demands for the dissolution of the tenure system have been made by faculty members concerned that the protection of tenured members will force the institution to sacrifice an opportunity to gain in quality because they feel a large proportion of younger staff are of a quality that would strengthen the institution.

At the same time, the promotion process may serve to strengthen the quality of promotions (and ultimately the institution), but at the cost of introducing a competitive relationship that current faculty find disruptive of collegiality.

Some of the same disruptions attend the introduction of greater numbers of off-tenure-track instructional staff on fixed contracts. If the assignment of faculty (tenure and tenure-track) is principally teaching, it is difficult to distinguish the assignments of tenured and tenure-track faculty and non-tenured instructional staff except through differential admission to governance procedures. Such a distinction may in itself heighten the sense of unfairness between two persons with similar responsibilities and credentials, one of whom has a probationary or tenured appointment and the other a relatively less secure fixed-term post.

The nature of the difficulties that both the disruption of lay-off actions and the procedures necessary to avert them may bring about suggests that the best approach to either is by intensive efforts to build a faculty consensus around a choice of alternatives.

If serious enrollment and concurrent budgetary loss is all but certain, only two alternatives exist for most institutions: reduce the number of permanent or long-term tenure commitments or lay off faculty when funds are insufficient. It is worth the effort to undertake almost any amount of consultation and study to build faculty understanding of and support for the first alternative. If a faculty prefers the second, however, and is committed to assuming responsibility for implementing it, a course that plans for layoff can, in principle, work. It would be of crucial importance, however, to assure that faculty thoroughly understand both the emotional reality and the institutional damage that is usually associated with layoffs of tenured staff.

Participation in the Layoff Process

Whatever the immediate cause—an institutional choice to lay off tenured faculty, a lack of planning, or a sudden and unpredictable loss of funds—an important number of institutions in the next decade will have to face the reality of abrogating appointment and tenure commitments.

The role played by the faculty may therefore be critical in determining whether the institution can minimize damage and even use the crisis to focus resources on the institution's strongest areas. But the question of consultation and faculty responsibility during decision making about who shall be laid off and what should be eliminated is a complex and hazardous matter. On the one hand, if faculty have held significant governance responsibility, that role is all but forfeited unless the faculty accepts major responsibilities in retrenchment decisions. Some faculties have done so (for example, the American Association of University Professors contract for the University of Cincinnati). On the other hand, most faculties have recoiled from such a role. This was generally the experience in institutions experiencing retrenchment in the UW System. And where the faculty is unionized, faculty unions generally urge their membership to stay away from such processes (Wakshull, 1978).

If faculty genuinely accept the responsibility to carry out necessary retrenchment, it is probable that some damage to the governance structure and fabric of life in the institution can be averted. But extensive discussion of alternatives before the extent of retrenchment is clear—without faculty assumption of responsibility—generates extremely high levels of anxiety and anger. Some administrations have minimized, though not eliminated, the disruption of a limited retrenchment by working out in detail what reassignments will be affected and what services will be curtailed before making public the need for retrenchment. The value of such a procedure is that uncertainty is minimized and only those actually affected suffer the expectation of job loss. The cost is that bitterness is likely to exist because the staff is shut out of discussions about a decision of great significance to their lives. Only the delicate balance of traditions and the nature of the staff's relationship to the administration and to governance responsibilities can determine which alternative should be taken.

Whatever the pattern of faculty-administrative consultative relationships, there are some practical administrative choices that may help when layoffs are inevitable.

Administrators should give careful thought, for example, to eliminating one or more whole functions, if possible, instead of cutting back every activity so that quality and morale are sacrificed institution-wide. Eliminating functions brings costs down faster because overhead as well as salaries diminish. It eliminates both unflattering discrimination among staff resulting from retrenchment on the basis of ability, and retrenchment of staff within a program solely on the basis of seniority without regard to ability. If planned well in advance, it may nonetheless be possible to place tenured members of the terminated program into other needed activities, while focusing the institution's resources on the thing needed most or done best.

It is also desirable to develop layoff procedures well in advance of need through a process that leads to as much internal consensus as possible and to make sure these procedures are known.

One such procedure should make it possible for faculty to leave campus with pay, if they wish, during a period of notice prior to layoff. Faculty who are unhappy and probably uncooperative, as will likely be the case, contribute substantially to lower morale and make it harder to rebuild after a fiscal emergency. A relocation leave with pay may be an advantage both to the individual and the institution.

Before retrenchment begins, administrators should work out in detail the legal steps for effecting actual layoffs. The text of written notices and the general content of conferences with affected staff should be cleared through a central office. Legal action following retrenchment is usually inevitable, and leaving each chairman or dean to improvise his own methods and written reasons may make it impossible to present evidence of fair and consistent action in court.

It is also important to have ready a procedure for assisting affected staff in relocating or assuming alternate activities when layoffs are announced, and to see that appropriate persons put real energy into helping them deal with this professional crisis. Despite the pressured atmosphere of a reduction in force, it is essential to maintain or create the opportunity to respond personally to individuals.

The administrator should, however, make sure that there is some procedure for ending the institution's layoff responsibility if the individual is no longer actively seeking reinstatement or has been offered a reasonably comparable alternate position. Otherwise, with the passage of time the institution may no longer know accurately its outstanding obligations.

Conclusions of the UW System Experience

In addition to the practical actions listed above, the most valuable, fundamental lessons to be learned include the need for sustained activity to assure institutional understanding of budgeting circumstances, to promote common values in evaluating choices, and to seek consensus in the selection of the methods with which to govern the university in financial hardship.

Some of those goals were achieved within the UW System after the layoffs of 1973-74 by an intensive consultative process to develop detailed retrenchment procedures. These procedures, developed by committees of faculty and faculty-administrators, with continuous legal help, were subsequently adopted by the regents as part of the faculty personnel rules. These rules form part of the Wisconsin Administrative Code (January 1975) and are enforceable as law. They were more detailed and extensive than similar provisions in any faculty collective bargaining agreement in four-year public institutions when reviewed in mid-1978. The emphasis of the rules is to guarantee faculty opportunity and responsibility for developing the direction and details of any retrenchment plan required to meet fiscal exigency. (A summary of the fifteen principal provisions of these retrenchment regulations appears in Figure 1).

Figure 1. Summary of Principal Provisions
of Retrenchment Regulations

The major elements of the retrenchment provisions (UWS 5, Wisconsin Administrative Code, *Register,* January, 1975, No. 229) are the following:
1. Establishes *criteria,* legally binding on the board, for the declaration of a financial emergency. Limits criteria to reduction of the general program operations budget of the institution and requires formal declaration of a financial emergency before retrenchment begins.
2. Provides for consultation with a standing faculty committee, chosen

as the faculty determines, *prior to* board consideration of a declaration of a financial emergency.
3. Provides for each institution's *faculty* as a whole to establish criteria to be used in conducting academic program evaluations and setting priorities in the event retrenchment is necessary.
4. Provides for *joint determination* by the institution's faculty committee (see 2 above) and its chancellor of recommendations to the board concerning:
   A. Existence of viable alternatives to reduction of filled positions, and
   B. Which colleges, schools, departments or programs shall be affected.
5. Requires submission of the committee report to the faculty senate and consultation with affected colleges, departments, and programs.
6. Guarantees opportunity for appearance by affected parties before the Board of Regents at an open meeting at the time the board acts on the recommendation presented by the faculty and chancellor with respect to a declaration of a financial emergency (see 4 above).
7. Rests "primary responsibility" for determining who shall be laid off on tenured members of the faculty of affected departments.
8. Establishes seniority as the criterion for layoff within each affected area of specialization, unless the faculty makes a "clear and convincing case . . . that program needs dictate other considerations."
9. Requires that evidence of the need for retrenchment and reasons for their selection be provided to faculty members with notification of layoff.
10. Provides a minimum of a twelve-month notice of layoff and guarantees that the appointment ends with the academic or fiscal year.
11. Provides for a due process hearing before a faculty committee on the appropriateness of the decision to lay off that particular faculty member and the submission of that faculty's determination to the chancellor.
12. Provides for final appeal to the board of the chancellor's decision if the committee reports that layoff was improper and the chancellor does not accept that determination.
13. Continues the layoff status for a tenured faculty member indefinitely unless that member resigns, accepts an alternate continuing position, or returns to the position from which laid off.
14. Guarantees reinstatement to any position having "reasonably comparable duties" in the institution from which retrenchment took place for three years from the date of layoff.
15. Uses the rule-making power of the Board of Regents to make the foregoing provisions part of the Wisconsin Administrative Code and thus subject to judicial enforcement.

Although none of these approaches can make fiscal austerity painless or desirable, in the right circumstances they can lead to a more thoughtful practice of matching goals to strengths and resources to needs.

References

Johnson, M. D., and Mortimer, K. P. *Faculty Bargaining and the Politics of Retrenchment in the Pennsylvania State Colleges 1971-1976.* University Park, Penn.: Center for the Study of Higher Education, the Pennsylvania State University, September 1977.

Karges, S. "Status Report: Tenured Faculty Layoffs." Letter to Wallace Lemon, July 10, 1980.

University of Wisconsin-System Total; Actual and Estimated Enrollments; Traditional Age Pool-Constant. Madison: University of Wisconsin, June 1978.

Wakshull, S. J. (State University of New York; President, United University Professions, AFT.) Public comments and panel discussion at sixth annual Conference of the National Center for the Study of Collective Bargaining in Higher Education, April 10, 1978.

Cyrena Pondrom has served as assistant to the chancellor, assistant chancellor (personnel), and vice-chancellor for personnel and analysis at the University of Wisconsin–Madison. She was responsible for developing UW System information about the impact of collective bargaining on four-year public institutions. In March 1979 she became the executive director of the governor's Employment and Training Office of the State of Wisconsin.

Based on recent experiences, the essays in this volume suggest lessons and strategies for the institutional researcher dealing with faculty reduction.

Conclusion: Developing a Process to Deal with Potential Faculty Reduction

Homer C. Rose, Jr.
Stephen R. Hample

Among the myths about higher education, one of the most mistaken —but most widely held—is the view that colleges and universities are "ivory towers," separated from "the real world." As the chapters in this volume indicate, higher education is very much a part of the real world and must adapt to market forces in order to retain stability. Anticipated enrollment shifts and diminishing public (real) expenditures will require that many institutions face the painful process of faculty reduction in the coming years; many others will escape cutbacks only through careful planning.

It has been the purpose of this volume to review the elements of the faculty reduction process, to share lessons from recent experience, and to suggest methods of approach to the problem. Each of the chapters has provided a different perspective on the issues; together they suggest a starting point for the institutional researcher who is faced with the prospect of retrenchment.

The Complexity of the Problem and the Need for Planning

The most powerful impression received from reading this volume is that the issues involved are complex and diverse; the best approach to faculty cutbacks will seldom be simple or straightforward. The nature of institutional problems and circumstances varies enormously. As a result, the procedures used to address cutbacks must also vary, incorporating different strategies and process participants. When cutbacks are required because of fiscal pressure, the extent of the financial difficulty primarily determines the scope of the problem, but many other factors must also be considered, including:
- Institutional size, complexity, and quality;
- Governance traditions and the strength of executive leadership;
- The nature of personnel and tenure systems or the existence of a unionized faculty;
- Sources of funding (for example, public or private),
- Previous experience with cutbacks.

These factors cannot readily be altered or controlled and must serve to constrain and direct retrenchment planning efforts. Each institution must examine its own resources and priorities through a process that recognizes its unique needs and circumstances. No single design, no matter how multidimensional, can reasonably hope to serve all institutions.

This limitation notwithstanding, the lessons of recent experience also suggest that careful planning serves to reduce the harmful effects of faculty reductions. As Pondrom notes, clear policies regarding retrenchment did help to make decisions more orderly and better related to future needs in the University of Wisconsin System, and as Dougherty notes, careful planning (leading to a series of well-executed program closures) allowed the State University of New York–Albany to respond both to gradual changes caused by enrollment shifts and sudden changes caused by financial pressure. Adequate planning can make a difference, and the basic components and issues of the required process can be identified. By addressing each issue, an institution can minimize the potential for unneeded, unfair, shortsighted, or unduly painful faculty reductions. Basic standards and warnings regarding faculty reductions are reviewed in this volume. This concluding chapter provides a summary of recommendations for beginning the recommended review process. Because institutional circumstances vary, only general principles can be offered. It is clear that careful planning is required, however, and that guidance for such planning is suggested by recent lessons.

Before reviewing the tasks required, two preliminary points should be noted.

1. Fundamental decisions for shaping a retrenchment planning process should be based on thorough review, be stated explicitly, and be clear to all concerned. These requirements can best be met through the development of written procedures either for an institution (such as those developed at the University of Michigan) or for a group of institutions (such as those developed for the University of Wisconsin System).

2. The first of these decisions is the designation of a reviewing group or person. Initially, the institution's board should be involved (since it is they, formally at any rate, who have authority to initiate and approve substantive changes). In practice, it is to be expected that an institution's chief executive officer will provide a recommended membership list for the review group; the board would then make the final determination. Membership probably ought to include at least one senior administrative officer and the senior institutional research or planning officer. Faculty representation should be considered and, if faculty are unionized, an opportunity should be provided for the involvement of a union representative. The most critical factor in determining membership of the review group, however, is that it must reflect the governance tradition of the institution.

Establishment of the Process

The review group should oversee the development of a planning and evaluation system through which to address the issues of retrenchment fairly and comprehensively. Such a system may also be useful for routine management purposes during times of stability. Nine basic tasks to address in this effort appear in the preceding chapters:

1. Development of a data base
2. Definition of circumstances necessary for retrenchment
3. Development of policies regarding participation
4. Examination of alternatives to retrenchment
5. Development of policies regarding program discontinuance
6. Review of role and mission statements
7. Review of legal standards and procedures

8. Assessment of political considerations

9. Distribution of policies and solicitation of comments

The completion of these tasks not only provides basic preparation for dealing with future faculty reductions with reasonable speed and comprehensiveness but may also provide the basis for an ongoing planning and evaluation process. Although each of the nine tasks is examined in earlier extended discussions, additional review is provided in this chapter as a summary reference source for the development of a retrenchment planning process.

It should be emphasized that the examination of these issues should be a *process,* not a single effort. As circumstances change or new information becomes available, it will be necessary to modify earlier efforts. Planning should always proceed from the most accurate and recent information available. An attempt has been made in the following review to discuss the required tasks in an appropriate sequence. Circumstances or other judgments, however, may rearrange the order in which the tasks are approached.

Development of a Data Base. Sound data are needed to address the issues of retrenchment. The institutional researcher must pay particular attention to this matter and should be centrally involved in the planning effort. Although data compilation can become overwhelming, ten comprehensive analyses or tasks are suggested. These constitute an ideal set upon which planners can draw, depending on campus characteristics and available time. Ideally, the planners should:

1. Examine current enrollments and project enrollments by level and discipline. They should also collect data regarding instructional activities by department, costs by department, costs of support facilities, and costs of all other non-instructional activities.

2. Use this information to create faculty profiles forecasting future needs for faculty by discipline and level. Faculty flow models (or at least some method for projecting faculty employment levels) are critical for all institutions, including those large enough to avoid layoffs through planning and the use of attrition. These data should include age patterns of faculty by rank, studies of faculty retirements by department, a study of older faculty (focusing on retraining for "optimum retirement activity"), forecasts of fringe benefits, the improvement of record keeping to assist "merit evaluation" systems, a determination of which faculty have other potential work outlets and which do not, an assessment of alternative retirement systems, and the development of joint efforts with personnel departments (for example, to develop data for pre-retirement or personal counseling programs).

3. Forecast the impact of faculty cutbacks on budgets, other departments, the tenure system, and enrollments.

4. Forecast the impact of alternate program eliminations on enrollments, other departments, the tenure system, and budgets (including overhead costs).

5. Begin routine collection of data required for legal purposes.

6. Design and conduct a study of campus atmosphere and morale to determine "if it contributes to creative teaching and productive research" (Harcleroad, this volume).

7. Develop and communicate basic information regarding the development and use of a system of "scientific" budgeting.

8. Organize the distribution of required information to designated personnel.

9. Provide data in support of efforts to develop institutionally specific definitions of "financial exigency."

10. Forecast trends likely to affect colleges and universities and assess trends in the educational needs of the region.

Definition of Circumstances Necessary for Retrenchment. Early in the development process, it is necessary to outline the conditions under which retrenchment must begin. The outline should include a definition (as explicit as possible) of what constitutes financial exigency and an indication of any other circumstances that would initiate active planning to reduce instructional activities or personnel. It is valuable to have formal, defensible criteria that must be met before any cutback process is initiated. Using information obtained in the preliminary effort to develop a data base, the researcher or planner can develop a precise outline of the extent of difficulty required to begin retrenchment. Ideally, the initiation of retrenchment planning will be based on definite needs that are clear to all. In Wisconsin, legally binding criteria of what constitutes a financial emergency are outlined in writing. Further, a formal declaration of a financial emergency (after consultation with a standing faculty committee) is required before the retrenchment process begins. This sort of procedure encourages openness and understanding, without which subsequent complications are invited.

Development of Policies Regarding Participation. It is not easy to address considerations of who shall have review authority, how and under what circumstances that authority may be delegated, and to whom (remembering the potential roles of external actors) it may be delegated. The related question of who shall participate (though without review authority) is no less complicated. Likely candidates, representing differing views and concerns, would include: state government officials, public policy agencies, institutional governing boards, institutional researchers, faculty (individually, by department, faculty senates, ad hoc review committees, peer review groups, tenure committees, faculty unions, and so on), students and student government groups, anti-cutback coalitions, media, local businesses and officials, deans, campus administrators, attorneys, and many more. The extremely complex human interplay involved in retrenchment review can make the process richer, more thorough, or more equitable, but not simpler. Apart from determining who shall have review authority and who shall be allowed to participate, a decision must be made regarding who shall receive what information—and at what stage of the process.

Unhappily, little guidance can be offered regarding the ideal mix of participation, but a few general observations may be made. Dolan-Greene suggests that full access to information should be provided at least to deans, administrative officers, and the board, and—depending upon circumstances—perhaps to faculty (individually, to the faculty senate, or the faculty union), students, the news media and others. She cautions, however, that if participation is too extensive, as in the Michigan DPP case, the process can become unduly complicated. The lesson drawn is that information should be more widely shared than opportunities for direct involvement if results are to be achieved and implemented efficiently.

It is clear also that faculty must be involved somehow (at least in peer reviews) and that if the faculty is unionized, the union must be given the opportunity to participate. In addition, if the faculty is not organized, and is not consulted prior to the retrenchment process, it is likely to unionize. Finally, however, since the issues of faculty reduction can cause extensive damage to weak faculty governance systems, participation under such circumstances should probably be minimized.

Whatever determinations are made regarding who shall decide, participate, and receive information, the decisions are most likely to be effective only if they reflect the governance tradition of the institution.

Examination of Alternatives to Retrenchment. It must never be forgotten that a critical preliminary exercise involves the continual and creative examination of alternatives to faculty reductions. Layoffs should always be a last resort. Although this point appears to be obvious, it can be overlooked. More commonly, however, the examination of alternatives is conducted too superficially and without creativity. When have all alternatives been exhausted? At a minimum, the examination should determine acceptable cutbacks in service and other non-instructional costs. It should take advantage of normal faculty attrition, examine early retirement programs, and attempt to design cooperative programs for alternative faculty employment. Also, an institution should ensure that the number of administrative personnel is as low as it can reasonably be before consideration is given to layoffs of instructional personnel. Finally, as Dolan-Greene notes, nonessential costs (for example, golf courses, conference centers) cannot be fully supported while faculty are laid off.

Even when the point of inevitable layoffs has been reached, alternatives must be examined, for instance, alternatives to the dismissal of faculty based only on seniority or to layoffs affecting strong and weak programs equally. Also, creative retirement schemes, placement services for faculty, retraining programs, or resignations in exchange for a year's leave with pay can be used to soften the blow of layoffs somewhat.

The range of alternatives available may depend upon institutional circumstances. Smaller institutions have less flexibility in this regard, since they cannot absorb faculty losses naturally (through attrition, for example) as easily as large institutions. In addition, institutions with a high percentage of tenured faculty are less likely to avoid layoffs (as opposed to "non-retentions" upon contract expiration) and complicated planning efforts.

Faculty themselves must plan for personal alternatives to their present jobs. The institution should try to retrain and relocate released faculty in support of these personal efforts. Early retirement planning that is well-coordinated, clear, and includes financial advice should also be considered.

Finally, in the design of any of these systems, the institution must remember to initiate a procedure for ending its responsibility when the laid off faculty member no longer seeks reinstatement or has been offered a reasonable alternative position. The institution must know its outstanding obligations.

Development of Policies Regarding Program Discontinuance. When alternatives have been exhausted, the planning group must approach the needed cutbacks with the needs of the entire institution foremost in mind. It is important to avoid widespread weakening of an institution in times of cutback if the necessary reductions can be made in weak or low priority programs. The welfare of the faculty—however important—is not synonymous with the welfare of the institution. The planner must serve the educational interests of students and the public through the most effective use of available resources in meeting the purposes of the institution. Although painful, the option of program cutback or discontinuance must be considered. The justification for such an approach is straightforward: If reductions are required, program discontinuance ordinarily better serves to maintain overall institutional quality (through the reduction of "unviable" programs) than do across-the-board cuts. The approach maintains productivity, retains most needed faculty (regardless of rank or tenure status), and can reduce overhead as well as salary costs (possibly reducing the total number of required faculty layoffs). If the number of required layoffs is extensive, program discontinuance may well be preferable to widespread cuts. It must also be recognized, however, that program discontinuance involves detailed, time-consuming, and emotional issues. In practice, it is often extremely difficult to include program discontinuance as a preferred retrenchment option.

If discontinuance of programs is considered, however, it is necessary to establish a program evaluation system (if one does not exist at the institution). The following elements should be included:

1. There should be an agreed upon procedure to conduct program analysis. Ideally, this procedure will already be established as the ongoing process of program review. If such an ongoing process does not exist, it should be established, since this sort of assessment will be an important management and planning tool in the coming years.

2. A decision must be made regarding the selection of programs for review; that is, basic criteria or rotating systems should be established. It would probably be wise to follow one of three methods: to evaluate all programs over a regular period of years, to target groups of related disciplines or programs together, or to select some strong and some weak programs for review. These procedures would serve to avoid the impression that selection for review automatically implies cutback.

3. A decision must be made regarding criteria for program reviews. If they are to be thorough, only a few program reviews should be conducted at a time. Reliance on easily available quantitative measures is inadequate. They may be used to select programs for review, but the inclusion of qualitative measures is preferred even at this stage. For the review itself, a combination of quantitative and qualitative measures should be used, and their application cannot be simplistic.

Review of Role and Mission Statements. Whether or not program discontinuance is considered as a retrenchment option, adequate institutional role and mission statements are imperative elements in the examination of faculty reductions. As Dougherty suggests, when decisions must be made regarding cutback or the elimination of programs, it is most desirable to reduce in areas that reflect least directly an institution's purposes or standards. Clear, meaningful role and mission statements—widely agreed upon and taken seriously—can allow the assigning of priorities to programs according to how well they serve primary institutional purposes. If existing standards are not clear and generally agreed upon, they should be improved; priorities should then be outlined. The use of role and mission statements in examining retrenchment questions can greatly assist in meeting goals of quality, particularly in institutions with strong academic reputations or those possessing sound faculty evaluation systems.

Review of Legal Standards and Procedures. Two basic legal considerations must be considered in preliminary planning efforts. First, if tenure or personnel practices are altered to discourage the widespread granting of tenure or other long-range commitments, care should be taken in the use of measures employed in the review, since that information will probably not remain confidential. Negative judgments in the tenure review process should not unfairly affect the ability of the faculty member (if laid off) to gain other employment. To the extent reasonable, tenure decisions should be based on objective criteria rather than personal evaluations.

The second issue concerns the selection of faculty for layoff and the provision of adequate due process. Reasonably consistent legal standards exist regarding proper institutional methods of selection for layoffs. Whatever method is followed, the standards employed to determine layoffs must be demonstrated to be neither arbitrary nor capricious. With a clearly developed program, careful review, and due process procedures, faculty reductions can be made with a minimum of legal difficulty. Planners should be able to demonstrate that the need for reductions was clear, that the method of selection for layoff was fair, and that the standards used to determine layoffs were shared with those affected. Each institution should also examine its existing due process procedures and make any changes required in order to meet court standards (see Hendrickson for detail). Finally, legal counsel should be consulted prior to the initiation of any retrenchment action, since legal requirements and liability standards vary by jurisdiction.

Assessing Political Considerations. As Dolan-Greene notes, diplomacy and political sophistication are required for any successful retrenchment effort. She advises that the planner not make decisions "in a political vacuum." No standard guidelines can be given regarding how best to achieve this end, but every effort should be made to anticipate political factors. The nature of this need may be demonstrated by recalling observations from the preceding essays. Externally, there will be little sympathy for laid-off faculty; internally, planners should expect (and prepare to deal with) anti-cutback coalitions, should expect local businesses to be concerned if cutbacks are large, and should be aware of legislators' interests.

Apart from predicting views of various interested parties, efforts should be undertaken to discourage faculty from hurting their own cause. The bickering or lowering of faculty or student standards—which may serve short-term purposes—will be counterproductive in the long run.

Finally, there is a likelihood of some form of public policy role in higher education's future planning efforts. The political implications of this prospect must be anticipated by institutional planners. Many other political considerations may also be expected. It is important to anticipate and develop strategies for response to political interests affecting the planning process.

Communication and Feedback. The design of a process to deal with faculty reduction can be fully effective only if there is widespread knowledge and agreement regarding standards and procedures. Some form of communication to the campus community, with an opportunity for comment, will assist campus planners to proceed with the understanding, if not the full support, of those affected.

Conclusion

This review of the basic components to consider in establishing a retrenchment planning process provides background for the design of institutional analyses that minimize the potential for repeating the mistakes of the past. The approach reviewed here is sufficiently comprehensive, but it can serve only as a beginning.

In many settings, careful planning will allow institutions to avoid cutbacks; others will not be able to avoid faculty reduction. In either case, the nature and effectiveness of management's efforts—and the degree to which those efforts meet the needs of all concerned—will depend in large measure upon the ability to recognize the particular factors important in a given setting and to develop and implement a thorough review process.

Suggestions for Further Reading

Chapter bibliographies in this volume provide primary references of additional information for the interested reader. Those sources include case studies of faculty cutback, formal institutional guidelines for retrenchment, reviews of retirement standards and policies, and the role of tenure in termination. Through these sources it should be possible to explore specific facets of the faculty reduction process in further detail. Apart from these sources, however, the literature on faculty reduction is not extensive, but a few additional sources should be mentioned:

Corwin, T. M., and Knepper, P. R. *Finance and Employment Implications of Raising the Mandatory Retirement Age for Faculty.* Policy Analysis Service Reports, Vol. 4, No. 1. Washington, D.C.: American Council on Education, 1978.

Although not the most recent exploration of the implications of Age Discrimination in Employment Act (ADEA) (see follow-up report by Corwin & Gross cited by Harcleroad), this report provides a useful analysis of the implications of the act upon costs of retaining older faculty and the number of young faculty members to be hired in the future. As stated in the report's synopsis, it has two sections: "(1) a summary of the data collected through a survey of colleges and universities; and (2) projections of the impact of the ADEA amendments on faculty employment and institutional compensation costs."

Furniss, W. T. *Steady-State in Tenure-Granting Institutions, and Related Papers.* Washington, D.C.: American Council on Education, 1973.

Although dated, this report contains useful discussions of the developments of staffing policies affecting faculty. Included are excellent explorations of alternative faculty patterns and factors affecting tenure and layoff. Included as appendices are the Association of American Colleges' "Statement on Financial Exigency and Staff Reduction" and the American Association of University Professors' "On Institutional Problems Resulting from Financial Exigency: Some Operating Guidelines."

Hample, S. R., and Kaelke, M. E. (Guest Ed.). *The Journal of the College and University Personnel Association,* 1980, *31* (1).

This issue of the CUPA journal consists of papers originally prepared for a sponsored symposium on "Future Faculty Employment: Projected Problems and Possible Solutions," held during August 1979. Included are several state level reviews of faculty reduction (Maryland, Minnesota, and California), institutional experiences (the universities of Montana, Colorado, and Wisconsin), and an excellent guide to relevant court cases.

Also included are a detailed review of Canadian faculty profiles, an organizational framework and comments on legislative actions contributed, respectively, by AIR members Bernard Sheehan, Marvin Peterson, and Paul Jedamus.

Patton, C. V. *Academia in Transition: Mid Career Change or Early Retirement.* Cambridge, Mass.: ABT Books, 1979.

    Patton presents a thorough review of early retirement systems and explores a range of alternative careers for faculty. Different approaches are developed to serve institutions of all sizes and circumstances.

Homer C. Rose, Jr., a recent graduate of the Center for the Study of Higher Education at the University of Michigan, formerly served in the Office of Institutional Research at Montana State University. He is now on the institutional research staff of the University of Michigan–Ann Arbor.

Stephen R. Hample is the director of institutional research at Montana State University and was formerly with the Maryland State Board for Higher Education. He recently directed a sponsored conference on future faculty employment problems and assisted the Montana Commissioner's Office in creating a statewide faculty development program.

Index

A

Academic quality issues: and program elimination, 11-12; in retrenchment and reputation, 43, 45-46
Administration, review of, 42, 44
Admissions, and enrollment trends, 3-4
American Association of University Professors (AAUP), 107; *Bulletin*, 12-13, 22-23, 28, 34; fiscal exigency guidelines, 123; at Oakland University, 51-53; policy statement on tenure, 28, 53-54, 86-87; review and censure process, 41; at University of Detroit, 57-58; at University of Michigan, 50
American Association of University Professors v. *Bloomfield College*, 28-30, 34
American Council on Education, 21
Angell, G. W., 61
Arnett v. *Kennedy*, 34
Asian Public Health Student Association, 49
Association of American Colleges, 123

B

Baldwin, R., 82, 94
Bardach, E., 10, 23
Bennett, B. J., 74-75, 77
Berdahl, R. O., 15, 23
Bignall v. *North Idaho College*, 32, 34
Blackburn, R. T., 83, 94
Black's Law Dictionary, 26-27, 34
Board of Regents v. *Roth*, 27, 31, 34
Board of Trustees. *See* Trustees
Bowen, H. R., 94
Bradley, A. P., Jr., 17, 23
Brenna v. *Southern Colorado State College*, 29-30, 32, 34
Brown, R. C., 27, 34

Browzin v. *Catholic University*, 28, 34
Budgeting: computer models for, 72-76, 117; and early retirement planning, 90-91; institutional research in, 66-74, 76-77; models for, 65-66; and program elimination, 10; recent trends in, 63-65

C

California, 85, 123
California, University of, 89; Berkeley School of Criminology closing, 11-12, 14, 16, 20-21; Riverside review process, 14
Cameron, J. M., 10, 23
CAMPUS computer model, 74
Canada, 123
Carnegie Council, 2
Caruthers, J. K., 66, 76-77
Cheit, E. R., 39, 61
Cincinnati, University of, 107
Clark, B. R., 79-80, 94
Clark, M. J., 17, 23
Collective bargaining contract, 3, 41, 60, 76. *See also* Faculty unionization
College and University Personnel Association (CUPA), *Journal*, 123
Colorado, 3, 71; University of, 123
Connecticut, 85
Cook, T. J., 85, 94
Corwin, T. M., 85-87, 94, 123
Cost data, 116-117; tabular forms of, 69, 71, 74
Courts. *See* Legal issues

D

Data collection: access issues of, 59-60, 118; for budgeting, 67-74; for evaluation of staff, 93; for faculty reduction, 59-60; on legal issues, 32-34; for retrenchment process, 116-117

125

Davis, C. K., 18, 23
Debus, R., 17, 23
Delaware, 85
DeLeon, P., 10, 23
Departments: and faculty layoffs, 30; interrelations of in retrenchment, 33, 73, 104
Detroit, University of, 40, 59-60; Academic Affairs Committee, 56; Board of Trustees, 55-56; Budget Planning Committee, 56; executive vice-president, 56; faculty lay offs at, 55-59; Senate, 56, 60; Vice President for Business and Finance, 56
"Developments Relating to Censure by the Association," 41, 61
Dolan-Greene, C., 37-61, 103, 118-119, 122
Dougherty, E. A., 9-23, 37, 66, 114, 121
Dressel, P. L., 17, 23, 77
Duerr, C. A., 34-35

E

Enrollments: and faculty dismissals, 4, 29-30, 33, 52; and faculty strategy, 6; and program elimination, 12, 39; projection of, 33, 52, 70, 76, 116-117; prospects for, 1, 3-4
Exxon Foundation, 11

F

Faculty: budget data on, 68-71, 116; career development stages of, 82-85; grievance process for, 39-42; modeling of needs for, 74-76; participation of in governance, 39-41, 55; participation of in retrenchment, 107-109, 117-118; part-time, 84, 88-89; and program elimination, 18-19; prospects for, 2, 123; as public employees, 3; reallocating positions of, 51-55; redeployment of, 83-85, 108, 124; reeducation of, 84; strategies for, 5-7, 117-119; work load data on, 33, 51-52, 55, 59, 63-64, 70. See also Retirement; Tenured faculty
Faculty layoffs: criteria for, 30-31; and enrollment trends, 4, 29-30, 33; individual responses to, 8, 119; institutional history of, 43-44; institutional research for, 37-38; legal issues on, 25-35, 121; at Oakland University, 51-55; participation in planning of, 107-109; procedures for, 7, 27, 31-32, 42, 115-118, 121; at University of Detroit, 55-58; at University of Wisconsin, 97-110. See also Budgeting; Legal issues
Faculty unionization: and information access, 60; at Oakland University, 51; and retirement issues, 86-87; and retrenchment process, 40-42, 115
"Financial Exigency and Reduction—In Force," 35
Financial exigency issues, 28-29, 92, 117; case law on, 29-33
Florida, 85
Flygare, T. J., 81, 94
Ford Foundation, 47
Formula budgeting, 71-72
Frances, C., 21, 23
Full-time equivalent measures (FTE), 63, 70, 74-75. See also Student-faculty ratio
Furniss, W. T., 123

G

Gault case, 81
Grany v. Board of Regents of the University of Wisconsin, 32, 35
Gross, A. C., 85, 94, 123

H

Halstead, D. K., 73-74, 77
Hample, S. R., 113-124
Harcleroad, F. F., 79-95
Hawaii, 85
Heim, P., 91, 94
Hendrickson, R. M., 25-35, 37, 59
Higher Education Price Index (HEPI), 73-74
Holloway, J. P., 35
Hughes, G. C., 94

I

Incremental budgeting, 67

Independent institutions. *See* Private institutions
Indiana, 4; University of, 89
Induced course load matrix (ICLM), 72-73
Information systems. *See* Data collection; Institutional research
Input evaluation, 17
Institutional governance: and retrenchment, 101, 114; and review process, 18
Institutional mission: and budgeting, 67; and program elimination, 13-14, 19-22; and retrenchment, 121
Institutional planning: and budgeting, 66; faculty in, 7; and retrenchment complexities, 114-115; and review process, 17, 114-117. *See also* Program planning
Institutional research: access issues in, 59-60, 118; for budgeting purposes, 66-74, 76-77; for faculty retirement and redeployment, 91-93; for legal purposes, 32-34; for program reduction, 9-11; in retrenchment process, 37-38, 58-61, 116-117. *See also* Data collection
Institutions: character of and retrenchment, 38-45, 79-80, 114; prospects for, 1-2; reputation of, 6; standards of, 6-7
Instruction costs data, 70-71, 116-117
Iowa Law Review, 26, 35

J

Jedamus, P., 123
Jenny, H., 91, 94
Jesuit order, 55-56
Johnson, M. D., 105, 111
Johnson v. Board of Regents of the University of Wisconsin System, 28-31, 35
Johnstone, W. A., 33, 37, 63-77
Jones, T., 80, 94

K

Kaelke, M. E., 123
Kaplin, W., 35
Karges, S., 99, 111
Kaufman, H., 10, 23

Kelly, E. P., Jr., 61
King, F. P., 85, 94
Kirschling, W. R., 1-8
Klein v. Board of Higher Education of the City of New York, 29-30, 32, 35
Knepper, P. R., 123
Krotkoff v. Goucher College, 28-30, 32, 35

L

Ladd, E. C., Jr., 83, 94
Legal issues, 108, 121; of due process, 27, 29, 31-33, 50; of financial exigency, 28-33; of liability, 32-33; in program elimination, 15; in retirement process changes, 90, of tenure contracts, 26-28
Lehmann, T., 17, 23
Lombardi, J., 84, 95
Louisiana, 16
Lozier, G. G., 41, 60-61

M

Maine, 85
Mandell, R. D., 45-46
Maryland, 123
Massachusetts, 85
Massachusetts Institute of Technology, 89
May, J., 23
Mayhew, L. B., 39-42, 58-59, 61
Media, 60. *See also* Public opinion
Melchiori, G. S., 10, 17-18, 23
Mentorship/sponsorship process, 83
Michael, D., 10, 23
Michigan, University of: Center for Population Planning, 50; "Discontinuance of Academic Programs" procedures, 18, 48-51; Office of Academic Affairs, 49-50; review at, 14-15, 115; School of Public Health, Department of Population Planning (DPP), elimination experience, 45-51, 59-60; speech and hearing program, 38-39
Michigan Educational Association (MEA), 58
Michigan State University, 51
Mingle, J. R., 13, 16, 23
Minnesota, 85, 123

Minority issues: cutbacks, 12, 49; and unions, 86
Mix, M. C., 40, 61
Montana, 64, 85; State University, 68, 72; University of, 123
Morale issues, and staff reduction, 93, 104-106
Mortimer, K. P., 105, 111
Mortimer, K. R., 40, 61
Mulanaphy, J. M., 82, 90, 95

N

National Board of Graduate Education, 16, 23
National Center for Higher Education Management Systems (NCHEMS), ICLM system, 72-73
National Educational Association (NEA), 57-58
National Endowment for the Humanities, 84
National Labor Relations Board (NLRB), 57
National Science Foundation, 83; Research Career Development Awards, 83-84; Research Scientist Awards, 84
New Hampshire, 85
New Jersey, 3, 71
New Mexico, 71
New York, 16; State Education Department, 12, 15; State University at Albany, 12, 15, 21, 114

O

Oakland University, 103; Academic Budget and Planning Committee, 53; Academic Policy Committee, 53; Academy of Dramatic Arts, 52-53; Classics Department, 53, 55; faculty reduction at, 51-55; Faculty Reemployment and Promotion Committee, 54; Modern Languages Department, 52, 54; Speech Communications Department, 53
Obetz, R. M., 84, 95
Objectives, strategies and tactics (OST) budgeting, 65-66
Ohio, 85
Orwig, M., 66-76, 77

Output evaluation, 17

P

Palmer, D. D., 87-88, 95
Palola, E. G., 17, 23
Parker, G., 82, 95
Patton, C. V., 87-89, 95, 124
Pennsylvania, University of, School of Allied Medical Professions, 13, 20, 22
Pension issues, 80-81, 89. See also Retirement
Pepper, C., 81
Perry v. Sinderman, 27, 31, 35
Peterson, M., 123
Pondrom, C., 97-111, 114
Presidents, and retrenchment process, 42-43
Private institutions, 87; and retrenchment process, 39, 80; and student aid allocation, 3-4; tenure in, 27
Process evaluation, 17
Productivity measures, 68-71
Program elimination: circumstances leading to, 11-14; guidelines for, 22; and institutional research, 9-11; nonacademic, 39, 73-74; policy development in, 119-120; process of, 17-19; at University of Michigan, 45-51
Program planning: faculty involvement in, 7; and faculty layoffs, 43; and public policy, 3; review process in, 14-17
Program planning and budgeting system (PPBS), 65
Program review: authority for, 14-15; dual systems of, 18; choice of programs for, 15-16; criteria for, 16; process of, 16-17, 120; quantitative and qualitative, 16
Public Health Student Association (PHSA), 49
Public institutions, 87; faculty layoffs at, 27-28; and retrenchment processes, 38-39; and student aid allocation, 3-4
Public opinion: and faculty layoffs, 5-6; and institutional support, 39
Public policy: shifting focus of, 2-5. See also States; U.S.

Q

Qualitative and quantitative review, 16

R

Rehmus, C. M., 40-41, 61
Research: budget data on, 68; and redeployment of faculty, 83-84
Research institutions, 87; and retrenchment, 45
Retirement, early, 80-82, 88-91, 124; and faculty career stages, 82-85; laws on, 85-87; systems of, 87-88
Retrenchment, 21; alternatives to, 118-119; defining circumstances of, 117; establishing processes of, 115-122; institutional research for, 37-38; 58-61; participation in, 117-118; planning for complexities of, 114-115; political realities of, 37-45, 122; review structure for, 114-117; strategies and experiences of, 45-58; Wisconsin regulations on, 109-110. *See also* Budgeting; Faculty layoffs; Program elimination; Retirement
Rhode Island, 85
Rolles v. *Civil Service Commission,* 35
Rose, H. C., Jr., 113-124
RRPM computer model, 74

S

San Francisco, University of, 40
Scheuer v. *Creighton University,* 28-29, 35
Schulman, C. H., 84, 95
Schultze, C. L., 77
Scully, M. B., 43, 61
Sheehan, B., 123
Shirley, R. C., 12, 23
South Carolina, 85
Southern Methodist University Institute of Technology, 77; *Annual Report,* 65-66
Stanford University, 89
State universities, 38, 50
States: budgeting and planning systems of, 64-65; education industry income of, 4; and faculty concerns, 3; priorities of, 13

Student Credit Hours (SCH), 69-71
Student-faculty ratio, 55, 59, 63-64, 70
Students: aid trends for, 3-4; budgeting data on, 68-73; changing profile of, 92-93; and faculty layoffs, 43-44, 60; minority, 12, 49; prospects for, 2; women, 12
Support programs, 39, 73-74

T

Tarule, J. M., 95
Teachers Insurance Annuity Association, 87, 91
Teaching Assistants Association, 102
Temple University, 43
Tenure contract, 25-26, 33; nature of, 26-28
Tenure issues, 40-41, 114, 123; and early retirement, 85-86
Tenured faculty: data collection on, 70; evaluation of, 90; and program elimination, 18; prospects for, 2; reduction of at University of Wisconsin, 101-102, 104-107; seniority of and layoffs, 30, 33, 43; termination of, 25-34. *See also* Faculty layoffs; Legal issues; Retirement
Texas, 71
Tierney, M. L., 40, 61
Trustees, 20; and faculty affairs, 3; and faculty reductions, 29-30
Two-year institutions, 88, 97

U

Unintegrated contracts, 26
Unions. *See* Faculty unionization
University of Detroit Professors' Union, 57-58
University of Wisconsin-System Total; Actual and Estimated Enrollments; Traditional Age Pool-Constant, 99-100, 111
U.S.: Age Discrimination in Employment Amendments, 1978, 81, 123; Agency for International Development (AID), 47; Congress, 81; Constitution, Bill of Rights, 27; Fourteenth Amendment, 25, 27, 29-31; Court of Appeals, 81;

Department of Labor, 85-86; population trends of, 80; Supreme Court, 27, 32

V

Volkwein, J. F., 12, 23

W

Wakshull, S. J., 107, 111
Washington State, 15
Weathersby, R. P., 95
Wildavsky, A., 23, 77
Wisconsin: Administrative Code, 109-110
Wisconsin, University of, faculty retrenchment, 31-32, 97-98, 114, 123; conclusions from flow models on, 100, 102-104; observations on, 100-101; personnel practices and, 101-102; regulations for, 109-110, 115; summary of, 98-100
Wisconsin State University, 101
Women: students, 12; and unions, 86
Wood v. *Strickland*, 32, 35

Y

Youn, T. I. K., 79-80, 94

Z

Zero-based budgeting (ZBB), 65-66